Discerning Liberative Motifs in Religions

Discerning Liberative Motifs in Religions

A Socio-Ecological Study

Lalchawiliana Varte

Christian World Imprints

First Published in 2020 by

Christian World Imprints
Christian Publishing & Books from India
C-3, Wazirpur Industrial Area
Delhi-110052
cwidelhi2017@gmail.com
www.ChristianWorldImprints.com
Phone: +91 11 41526079

ISBN: 978-93-5148-459-2 (HB)
ISBN: 978-93-5148-460-8 (PB)

Printed in India.

Contents

Foreword

In the midst of Covid-19 Pandemic and rapid rise in number of positive cases, the Lockdown order from the National and State authorities followed by sit at home period has been fruitfully utilized by the author of this book, Rev. Lalchawiliana Varte. While the pens and computers of many authors are locked down, the hands of this author have been constantly working to bring to us the necessity of focusing on religion in general and several religious traditions in particular, supplying us with liberative lessons through the selected topics. The book opens our eyes in order to see the value of having various faith traditions as they deal with the needs of humankind in their respective ways and perspectives.

In a world plagued by fundamentalism, communalism, ecological crisis, oppression and suppression, religion has proved to be a strong catalyst that has been maneuvered and exploited by certain sections of society to fulfill their self-centered purposes. However, every religion has the prospect to be liberative and has the influence to bring about transformation in the society. In order for this to become a reality, followers of every religious tradition must realize the liberative motifs present in religious traditions. What this book strives to achieve is to make the readers discern the liberative strands that are present in some major religions and thereby appreciate the diversity of life and faith. This does not entail a giving up of one's own faith tradition. Appreciation does not necessarily lead to conformation, rather appreciation leads to respect and understanding. Therefore, a realization and appreciation of the liberative motifs in religious traditions other than one's own tradition can lead to transformation of one's mindset and worldviews while still holding on to the traditions that one holds so dear.

I wish each and every reader of different sides to get insightful knowledge contained in this volume as it would give them great academic profit as well as spiritual enrichment. I want to express my joyful appreciation to this young theologian who has become a prolific writer in the field of Religions due to his untiring efforts.

(Prof. T. Vanlaltlani)
Adjunct Professor
Department of Religions
Aizawl Theological College
Mizoram

Preface

Religion, a potent unifying force as well as an intoxicating divisive agent, at the same time, has often been exploited by nefarious agents to fulfill their selfish needs. However, it must be reiterated that religion itself is not an agent of oppression or exploitation. It is simply an agent, an instrument in the hands of despicable individuals and systems. Therefore, the need of the hour is to discern the liberative elements that are present in all religious traditions of the world. Religion alone might not be enough to address all the various socio-economic, political and ecological problems plaguing the world. However, religion because of its strong emotional appeal has the potentiality to change worldviews, perspectives and mindsets. Therefore, religion has the power to enable individuals to be agents of change and transformation in society.

Theological education, especially the study of religions can have a great impact on worldviews and perceptions. It can facilitate students to appreciate the positive elements and teachings prevailing in other religious traditions. However, this does not indicate that students of religion are generally pluralistic or syncretistic. The study of religions can help students to be critical of their own faith traditions in order to strengthen and edify their own faith and traditions more and more. Thereby, they can be enabled to synthesize liberative elements present in religions in order to bring about sociological and ecological transformation.

Therefore, this humble work which is a collection of some of my articles and seminar papers endeavours to bring out the richness and beauty in diversity of life through a study of liberative elements found in some of the major religious traditions. It is my fervent hope that through this modest work we may be able to in some way appreciate what is good and true in other faith traditions. When we learn to appreciate and comprehend the liberative elements present in other faith traditions, then we will be able to understand diversity as a gift of God that is to be enjoyed and not a threat to identity or faith, only then shall we be able to lead happier, peaceful, harmonious lives.

I would like to take this opportunity to acknowledge my utmost gratitude to all the people who have been instrumental in helping this work see the light of day.

My heartfelt appreciation goes to all the theological teachers who have helped me to shape my thoughts and views; especially the teachers of the Religion department at Aizawl Theological College, who have been especially influential in inspiring me to undergo the study of religions and have facilitated me to comprehend the liberative elements present in all religions.

My sincere gratitude goes to my family: my mother Mrs. Sangthuami, my sister Laltanpuii Varte, my wife Mrs. Lalsiamthari Varte and our children David Vanlalhruaia Varte, Anna Lalremruati Varte and Noel Malsawmtluanga Varte, who have provided me with the strength and endurance to victoriously face the battles of life.

I am also extremely grateful to Prof. T. Vanlaltlani, Adjunct Professor, Aizawl Theological College, Department of Religions, who graciously consented to write a Foreword of the book. I am indebted to Prof. T. Vanlaltlani who has been a patient and enlightening guide and mentor for me all throughout my theological journey.

My heartfelt gratefulness once again goes to Mr. Sudhanshu Kanda and his colleagues at Christian World Imprints, New

Delhi, who in the midst of immense hardships displayed massive enthusiasm and worked tirelessly in order for this modest work to materialize.

Finally, I thank the Almighty who called me into this Ministry of Grace and enabled me to appreciate what is good and true in others and thereby realize the beauty of life. May all glory and honour be to God alone.

Lalchawiliana Varte

Chapter 1

Defining Religion and the Need of Recouping Religion

Defining Religion…'Religion' is a term often used, but often understood differently and very often misinterpreted and misused. Although many have attempted to define the phenomena of 'religion,' we can say that no one has given a single definition of 'religion' that has been unanimously accepted all over the world. However, some of the attempts at defining religion made by scholars may be mentioned as follows:[1]

- ✓ **Schleirmacher:** Religion is feeling of absolute dependence.
- ✓ **William James:** The enthusiastic temper of esposal.
- ✓ **Emile Durkheim:** Religion is a unified system of beliefs and practices relative to sacred things, that is to say things set apart and forbidden, beliefs and practices

[1] T. Vanlaltlani, *Tribal Religion: Mizo and Bru* (Aizawl: Mizo Theological Association, 2009), 8. Hereafter cited as T. Vanlaltlani, *Tribal Religion*…

which unite into one single moral community called a church all these adhere to.

- ✓ **Rudolf Otto:** The essence of religious awareness of awe, a unique blend of fear and fascination before divine.
- ✓ **Max Muller:** Religion consists in the perception of the infinite under such manifestations as are able to influence the moral character of man.
- ✓ **E. B. Tylor:** The belief in spiritual beings.
- ✓ **A. B. Tirkey:** Religion is an attitude of mind, something that may be described in an ascending scale of spirituality as fear, awe, reverence, admiration and love of what is indescribably beautiful, good and holy.
- ✓ **T. Vanlaltlani:** Religion is an unseen powerful force controlling over the life of a person or a community due to individual or community's faith in such supernatural power-holder who may be called God, Sacred, Holy Other; Pathian or any other.

Therefore, we can say that religion is the phenomena that human beings believe to have an impact on our lives and even upon after death. Our beliefs, patterns of worship, faith and various traditions can all be included within the sphere of religion.

The Need of Recouping Religion... Religion, in many aspects a uniting factor for humankind can also be a cause of disunity and a major obstacle to unity and peace as it creates group mentality which in turn creates selfishness. Moreover, zeal for the propagation or safeguarding of one's religious beliefs can also be the cause of violence and bloodshed. Religion because of its strong emotional appeal can be utilized and manipulated for the instigation of violence in different forms. It has been used to reinforce self-centered attitude or superior conceit among the devout believers, while the people of other faiths are considered as evil. Furthermore, the extreme fondness to religion can also contribute to strong conviction that holds anything is acceptable for the glory of religion; even violence and bloodshed. Additionally, religion has been used to justify gender injustice as well as the wanton destruction of the ecological system by humankind for their selfish greed.

However, it must be understood that religion per se is not responsible for the various maladies that are perplexing the world. Rather it is the exploitation of religion for self-centered considerations of power, privilege and selfish greed that has resulted in the present appalling scenario. Religion from a significant devotion has been turned into an irrational obsession. It is no longer a vision of life; it is being made to serve as a deceitful strategy. It is no longer an instrument of healing, unity or peace. It is not a mission for establishing a just world but a medium for the augmentation of the elite few.

Therefore, in today's context, followers of every religious tradition must be made aware that much of our perspective towards religion and the way we frequently utilize religion often betrays the fundamental beliefs of that tradition. Therefore, religious traditions must be ready for a self-criticism of what has been going under the name of religion. There is a pertinent need to recoup religion so that it once again becomes an agent of healing, a cohesive factor that binds together people of every caste and creed, race and faith.

Discerning Liberative Motifs in Religion... In this situation, the most viable solution seems to be appreciating the liberative motifs that are present and found in religious traditions by followers of all faiths and thereby a forging of unity of these liberative strands. By strengthening the liberative core of religion, antidotes to various ailments that are ailing the world can be developed. Liberative aspects or elements are present and found in every religious tradition. To uphold those elements is one of the important measures to counter the problems that the world is facing. In order to further this process, the following assertions may be made:[2]

- ✓ A belief in a God of Justice who loves all people.

[2] John S. Augustine, ed., *Religious Fundamentalism: An Asian Perspective* (Bangalore: SATHRI/CCA/WARC, 1993), 186.

- ✓ Recognition of Diversity as a gift of God which should be viewed as enriching experience and not as a threat.
- ✓ A dialogical understanding of Truth/God rather than exclusivist claims.
- ✓ A relationship of tolerance and equal respect among people of different faiths.
- ✓ Endeavoring to build a society where men and women are treated equally and where there is no discrimination/ exploitation on the basis of sex, family status/economic background, etc.
- ✓ Building one human community in which separate identities are honored and homogenized.
- ✓ An affirmation of the absolute worth of life and the formation and sustaining of structures to protect this.
- ✓ Inculcating, developing and perpetuating a wholesome respect and care for Nature and the whole of God's creation.

Every religion has the inner potential for change. Religion becomes liberative when it breaks forth from the narrow dogmatic fundamentalistic garb and meets all the people, particularly the poor and the oppressed. Religion has the responsibility of becoming protest movements against structures, systems, beliefs and practices, which oppress, exploit and marginalize people. Therefore, recouping religion is a pertinent duty that devout individuals of all religions need to pursue in the present context.

However, discerning liberative motifs in religions requires us to appreciate diversity of faith which begins with a critical evaluation of our own faith traditions and demands appreciation of dogmas, doctrines, creeds and worldviews that are totally different from what we hold on to. It requires us to have a speculative view of what we intensely hold dear. It insists of us to drop the superiority attitude that we have towards other faiths. So, the very pertinent question in appreciating diversity of faith is: "Are we ready to be critical of ourselves?"

Role of the Church: The Church should commit itself to proclaiming a firm conviction that violence and terrorism are incompatible with the authentic spirit of religion, and condemn every type of violence perpetrated in the name of religion. The Church has to teach the people of different faiths that the riots, brutal killings, discriminations on the grounds of gender, caste or creed, wanton and selfish destruction and exploitation of nature are not the answer to the problems and differences. The Church needs to work as a mediator and play an important role in the local, national and international level. It should motivate, educate and encourage the members of the congregation to actively participate in the liberation of the oppressed and the marginalized.

The evangelization of the world should not be concerned only with spiritual salvation, but to transform the world, to change the economic, socio-political, cultural and religious milieu. The Church should work for the realization of the Kingdom of God in the here and now and the inculcation of Kingdom values in the society. There is a need to work for unity among the various religious and cultural traditions through dialogue, which provides the creative challenge for introspection, growth and insight within our own faiths and traditions also.

Thus, religion, which occupies a pivotal position in the lives of human beings because of being manipulated, misinterpreted and misrepresented needs to be recouped. In order to do this, we need to discern the liberative motifs present in religions which demands an appreciation of diversity, of faith, beliefs and traditions. Then religion shall once again become an agent of transformation, a healing balm in Gilead from whence people and the entire creation can receive healing (Jer. 8:22).

Chapter 2

Re-Reading Tribal Myths & Folklores for Socio-Religious Transformation A Study of the Biate Myth of Fapite

Although, several terms have been used to describe the traditional religion of the tribals, it has commonly been referred to as 'Primal Religion.' It does not have a written scripture. But, they have myths and legends, folktales and stories in which their whole religious ethos is embodied. These have been handed down orally from generation to generation. The richness of tribal oral tradition has been beautifully described by Renthy Keitzer, who calls it the unwritten "Prime Bible" by writing the following words:

> These (oral traditions) may be called as the unwritten 'Prime Bible' of the tribal/indigenous people. One can find in these oral traditions their beliefs, norms, and practices; hence a great and rich treasure of theological value is hidden with this 'Prime Bible' of the people.[3]

[3] Renthy Keitzer, *In Search of a Relevant Gospel Message* (Guwahati: CLC, 1995), 85.

Wati Longchar understands these myths as the ground of religion and that they contain the religious truth of a particular community. Myths teaches how the Supreme Being works and reveals the Divine mysteries through creation, the place of the human, and the animal kingdom in this universe, their relationship and so on.[4] Thus, myths may be considered as the sacred Scripture and creed of the tribals.

Myths convey profound theological meanings and the religious truth of a particular group of people. They tell us about God, spirits and their relations with human beings and creation. They tell us how human beings understand themselves, their life realities and their relationship with God and creation.[5] Thus, myths understood under the right perception can give wonderful insights for enriching the moral standards of the tribal people.

Here an attempt is made to evaluate and re-read a particular tribal myth, the Biate myth of Fapite to be precise, in order to find out its various socio-religious significances.

1. Different Terms Used for Referring 'Primal' Religion

In ancient times people used to practice the so-called primal religion through their practical life without any consciousness of their cultural and racial unity or identity. But, historical events and modern developments have awakened the consciousness of the primal people raising questions relating to race, culture and religion.[6] Since the term 'primal' has several connotations some of which are negative and derogatory, it is not suitable to call the practitioners of such a religion as 'primal people.'

---

[4] A. Wati Longchar, "Myth: A Source for Conceptualising Tribal Theology," in *An Exploration of Tribal Theology* (Jorhat: The Tzudikong Baptist Church, 1997), 83. Hereafter cited as Longchar, *Myth...*

[5] Yangkahao Vashum, "Sources for Developing Tribal Theology," in *An Exploration of Tribal Theology*, edited by Wati Longchar (Jorhat: The Tzudikong Baptist Church, 1997), 66-67. Hereafter cited as Vashum, *Sources...*

[6] T. Vanlaltlani, *Tribal Religion...*, 8.

A number of terms have been employed to deal with primal religion. Such as:[7]

a) **Primitive:** The term 'primitive' has been used by Presler and others for dealing with primal religion. But, in the opinion of scholars like Suresh Sharma and others, it can have a pejorative or demeaning connotation because the practitioners of primal religion are not necessarily primitive or backward.

b) **Indigenous:** This term is too broad; therefore it does not necessarily mean primal society.

c) **Natives:** This term, on the other hand is too narrow as it is more prevalent in American countries and some parts of Europe like the United Kingdom. Therefore, it is not relevant for the study of primal religion.

d) **Folk:** This term generally connotes the common people differentiated from the elite class of society. Such societal distinctions do not exist in the primal society.

e) **Aborigines:** This term specifically refers to the original inhabitants of Australia, therefore it is too exclusive.

f) **Adivasi:** This term commonly refers to the tribals of mainland India; therefore it is also too exclusive.

g) **Archaic:** This term refers to the ancient and uncivilized people and their religion. But, the primal people as well as their religion are living and dynamic. Therefore, this term is also not relevant in the study of primal religion.

Thus, as of now, there is no appropriate term for describing the religion of indigenous people and those practicing their traditional or original religion. Due to the unavailability of any satisfactory term, the expression 'primal' seems to be the most suitable word for now. In attempting to define primal religion, it may be defined as the traditional religion of the original inhabitants or indigenous people of a particular area; a religion with a pre-scientific worldview and having no rigid boundaries between the spiritual and secular dimensions of life, relying more on oral

---

[7] T. Vanlaltlani, *Tribal Religion...*, 9-11.

traditions than written scripture and enacting myth in rituals and sacrifices.

However, here, the terms 'primal religion' and 'tribal religion' are used interchangeably.

2. Main Characteristics of Primal Religion

In brief, primal religion is the religion practiced by the tribals. Tribal religion through the centuries has been equated with the terms such as animism, preliterate, primitive, and primal. Other names such as animatism, spiritism, ancestor worship and fetishism have also been employed to explain tribal religion. Besides these, as has already been explained, the term 'Primal Religion' has also been used extensively and is a widely accepted term, especially in India.[8]

The particular term 'Primal Religion' has been championed by Prof. J. H. Thumra who asserts that, "when we study the religion and practices of the tribal people we will find that many of the basic features of these people are basic or primary in the religions of the world."[9] Therefore, the term "Primal Religion" seems to be the most appropriate term as of now to refer to the living and dynamic religions of the tribal people.

The main characteristics of the Tribal/Primal Religion may be enumerated as follows:

a) **It is a Community Religion:** A unique characteristic of tribal religion is that, it is principally a community religion. In a tribal community, a person must actively participate in the beliefs, ceremonies, rituals and festivals of the community, in order to be truly human and to belong to the entire community as well as with the ancestors and all of creation. It is impossible for a person to live all alone in isolation from the community.

---

[8] Tirkey, *Religion...*, 168-169.

[9] Jonathan H. Thumra, "The Primal Religious Tradition," in *Religious Traditions of India,* edited by P. S. Daniel, David C. Scott and G. R. Singh (Delhi: ISPCK, 2001), 45-46.

Therefore, in the tribal religion, an individual's life and the community are inseparable.[10]

Moreover, tribal religion is the innumerable rites and rituals that begin from the womb till death which leads to the afterlife. Therefore, as asserted by Dr. Longchar, in order to understand the core of tribal religion, one has to understand the religious journey of the individual that begins from the womb till the time of physical death and continues to the hereafter. Furthermore, for the tribals, belief and action cannot be separated; they belong to one single whole. Worship and action go hand in hand. Religion is action. That means without belief and action, one cannot understand the religious meaning of the tribals.[11]

b) **Value of Oral Tradition:** The other distinctive characteristic of the tribal religion is the absence of sacred scripture/scriptures like other religions. The religious ethos is contained in the hearts and minds of the community and in the oral history and rituals. In a sense, the community itself is a living sacred scripture.[12] Nirmal Minz also asserts that, in a tribal religion, there is an absence of any written scripture. It is the religion of oral traditions, of corporate 'memory' passed on from generations. Religious rituals, teachings and principles are transmitted orally from one generation to another.[13]

Moreover, for the tribals, creation is a manifestation of the Supreme Being. Tribal religion cannot be truly

---

[10] A. Wati Longchar, *The Traditional Tribal Worldview and Modernity* (Jorhat: Eastern Theological College, 2000), 6. Hereafter cited as Longchar, *The Traditional ...*

[11] Longchar, *The Traditional ...*, 6.

[12] Longchar, *The Traditional...*, 7.

[13] Nirmal Minz, "The study of Tribal Religion in India," in *Re-visioning India's Religious Traditions: Essays in Honour of Eric J. Lott*, edited by David C. Scott & Israel Selvanayagam (Delhi: ISPCK, 1996), 122. Hereafter cited as Minz, *The Study of...*

understood without creation. The people see the self of the Supreme Being in creation and the Supreme Being speaks to them through creation. Therefore, for the tribals, creation is a part of scripture.[14]

c) **Absence of Founder(s)/Reformer:** Another distinctive characteristic of the tribal religion is that unlike other religions of the world, it does not have a founder or a reformer. In other words, their religion is not centered on great historical person/persons. Instead, their religion is earth/creation centered. It is true that the tribals have a tradition of divine birth and manifestations, but they are not worshipped. Religious functionaries, famous men and women also exist, who are highly esteemed and respected, and they form an integral part of the religious setting, but they are in no way worshipped or venerated as divine representatives.[15]

d) **Absence of Permanent Place of Worship and Idols:** No human-made images or temples are used for worship of the Divine. Natural objects are accepted as symbols of the divine presence and adoration and oblations are given seasonally. Life-cycles, birth, marriage and death, and annual cycles of major seasons and changes of nature accordingly form an integral part of occasional and seasonal festivals and scarifies.[16] Although, as pointed out by Tirkey, among the Oraons, there is a common spot known as *chala, jaher,* or saran, the sacred grove, while the Mundas have *adding* as an abode for their ancestor spirits, which they care for and offer sacrifices to their ancestors at this very place. Except for these two spots of offering sacrifices, there is no man made place of worship in the tribal religion. Worship or sacrifices are done at homes, village roads, graveyards, fields

[14] Longchar, *The Traditional...,* 6.

[15] Longchar, *The Traditional ...*, 7.

[16] Minz, *The Study of...*, 122.

etc.[17] Although, temporary altars for offering sacrifices are to be found among the tribal people, there is no permanent place of worship since they believe that God can be worshipped anytime and anyplace, for God is not limited to any place. Thus, the whole earth is a place of worship for the tribal people.

e) **Ancestor Worship:** According to Nirmal Minz, another important characteristic of Tribal religion is the worship of ancestors. The ancestors are part of the life of those who are alive and they are interested in the welfare of the living.[18] The ancestral spirits are invoked for help and welfare of the living members of the clan. They are offered a few grains of rice at each meal. At all the major feasts and festivals they are offered a portion of each item of the meal and in the name of the departed ancestors a few drops of rice beer are first offered.[19] Among the Mizos of Mizoram, *Mim Kût*, celebrated in the month of *Mim Kût Thla* (i.e., September), was an agricultural festival in which the first fruits of the fields were offered, especially in honor of the dead.[20]

The tribal people believe that the spirits of the ancestors never depart from the family members and continue to live with them in the form of spirits. It is also believed that the spirits of the ancestors come and help and also share in all difficult moments in the lives of the living members of the family. Therefore, ancestor worship forms an integral part of the tribal religion.[21] Thus, for the tribals they are separated from their ancestors only in form and their relationship continues after death. For that reason, their

---

[17] Tirkey, *Religion...*

[18] Minz, *The Study of...,* 122.

[19] Tirkey, *Religion...,* 184.

[20] T. Vanlaltlani, *Tribal Religion...*, 67.

[21] A. Wati Longchar, *The Tribal Religious Traditions in North East India: An Introduction* (Jorhat: Eastern Theological College, 2000), 20. Hereafter cited as Longchar, *The Tribal...*

established relationship with their ancestors continues in terms of offering by the living members for the departed ones.

Besides the above mentioned characteristics of the tribal religion, it may be mentioned that there is no clear distinction between the sacred and the profane in the tribal religion. Their religious life and their social life are interrelated and intertwined in an inseparable way. Moreover, primal religions provide all seeds of world religions. Although, this is only a theory and there is no proof to believe this kind of Darwinian Theory. But, in the primal religion we find elements of the major religious traditions, such as the belief in Supreme Being, belief in life after death, etc.

3. Myths and Folklores in Primal Religion

Myths and Folklores play an important role in the formation of the beliefs and practices of the tribals. Since the tribals do not have any written scripture to provide a systematic description of their worldview, their whole religious philosophy is implanted in myths, oral history and rituals. Therefore, myths and folklores are the scriptures and creeds of the tribal people. Before going further, let us look at the meaning of these two terms.

The term "folklore" was coined by W. J. Thomas in 1846, prior to this, it was known as "popular antiquities." It has been derived from the German word '*Volklehre*' which means, people's customs. In anthropological usage the term folklore has come to mean myths, legends, folk-tales, folk-songs, proverbs, riddles and a variety of forms of artistic expression whose medium is the spoken word.[22] Folklore generally refers to the body of material, in a variety of forms that expresses the traditions of a particular culture. Folklore is the body of expressive culture, including tales, music, dance, legends, oral history, proverbs, superstitions, and so forth, common to a particular population, that comprise the traditions of that culture, subculture, or group.[23]

---

[22] L. P. Vidyarthi and Binay Kumar Rai, *The Tribal Culture of India* (New Delhi: Concept Publishing Company, 1976), 309. Hereafter cited as Vidyarthi and Rai, *The Tribal Culture*...

[23] http://www.newworldencyclopedia.org/entry/Folklore (July 16, 2013).

Myth has been defined as, a usually traditional story of ostensibly historical events that serves to unfold part of the world view of a people or explain a practice, belief, or natural phenomenon.[24] For Mircea Eliade myth is, "a true story and, beyond that, a story that is a most precious possession because it is sacred, exemplary, significant."[25] Presler has also defined myth as, "a story of religious import, especially an account handed down by tradition, of the activities of supernatural beings."[26] Whereas, for Dr. T. Vanlaltlani, myths are, "the stories by which people express what they believe about the world in which they live and they are the fruit of people's thinking about the way life is, and why things happen as they do."[27] Therefore, we can say that a myth is a story which is valuable for a community, handed down orally from one generation to another, and which gives an account of the beliefs and practices of the people.

Thus, myths may be considered as the sacred Scripture and creed of the tribals. They convey profound theological meanings and the religious truth of a particular group of people. They tell us about God, spirits and their relations with human beings and creation. They tell us how human beings understand themselves, their life realities and their relationship with God and creation.[28] Thus, myths understood under the right perception can give wonderful insights for enriching the moral standards of the tribal people.

4. Who are the Biates?

The Biate community is a small but distinct people who belong to an old hill tribe of the great Chin-Kuki-Mizo group of the Indo-Mongoloid stock of race. They are found mainly in Dima Hasao

---

[24] http://www.merriam-webster.com/dictionary/myth (July 16, 2013).

[25] Mircea Eliade, *Myth and Reality* (London: George Allen and Unwin Ltd., 1963), 1.

[26] Henry H. Presler, *Primitive Religions in India* (Bangalore: The Christian Literature Society, 1971), 72.

[27] T. Vanlaltlani, *Tribal Religion*..., 205.

[28] Vashum, *Sources*..., 66-67.

district of Assam, India and the Saipung Constituency of Jaintia Hills of Meghalaya in India.[29] Though they are less in terms of population they have their own identity with a rich and distinctive history, culture, dialect and religious heritages. They are also one of the oldest tribes living in the North East India especially among the Chin-Kuki-Mizo family.[30]

According to legend, the Biates were the descendents of *Manmasi* and consider that they have originated from a place called *Khurpui*, sometimes also known as *Sinlung*. With regards to the place and time of their sojourn from *Khurpui* or *Sinlung*, nothing concrete can be known as there is no evidence. The Biates of Dima Hasao and Jaintia Hills are the people who came from the Champhai valley of Southwest Mizoram via Tripura (Tipera) kingdom. The Biates are known to be the first settlers of Mizoram.[31]

K. Zawla, a Mizo historian also emphatically states that, the Biates were the first to set foot on the soil of Mizoram and their glory days in that land was about until the 15th Century C.E.[32] In the same vein, J. Shakespear also says that, the Biates claim the hills around Champhai as their place of origin, and the sites are still known by their names.[33] The Biates had been forced to leave the *Sakram* (Southern Mizoram) due to the rebellion of the great *Pois* known as *Pawi Rallian* or *Pawi iral* which means Great Pawi Rebellion sometime in the last part of the 15th Century C.E.[34]

With regards to the origin of the name 'Biate,' according to one tradition, while the Biates were in the Saitual region of

---

[29] Ramdina Lalsim, *Tribes of N.C. Hills, Assam* (Haflong: Cultural and Publicity Officer, N.C. Hills Autonomous Council, Haflong, Assam, 2005), 63. Hereafter cited as Ramdina Lalsim, *Tribes...*

[30] http://ezralalsim.blogspot.in/2011/01/biate.html (29 July 2013).

[31] Ramdina Lalsim, *Tribes...*, 63-64.

[32] K. Zawla, *Mizo Pi Pute leh an thlahte Chanchin* (Aizawl: K. Zawla, 1964), 17.

[33] J. Shakespear, *The Lushei Kuki Clans Part I* (Aizawl: Tribal Research Institute, 1975), 6.

[34] Ramdina Lalsim, *Tribes...*, 69.

Mizoram, some Biate villagers used to appease the *Rulpui* (python) by offering animals. Later on the python began to demand human sacrifice and the villagers used to appease the python by offering a child annually.[35] Thus the word 'Bia-te' originated from this legend, as '*Rul-bia-te*' which means 'snake worshippers.'[36] However, majority of the Biates reject this interpretation regarding the origin of the word Biate.

5. The Myth of *Fapite*: Queen of the Paddy[37]

Once upon a time, there was a village in which the whole villagers were informed that the rich and famous Queen of *Siset* would pay a visit to their village and to prepare themselves to welcome the Queen by cleaning their respective houses and the surroundings. The whole village prepared to welcome the great chief eagerly. In the meantime, instead of the much awaited Queen, an old woman with her shabby dress entered their village and asked everyone if she could pass the night there (in fact, the Queen was in the form of an old woman to test the virtue of the villagers). But, no one cared for the old woman, except the poorest orphan of the village *Liandoia* who welcomed the hapless old woman and offered her the little amount of rice he had. The old woman learnt that the rice she had been offered was all that *Liandoia* had, and that he was the only person in the whole village that had kindness, love and compassion for others. Therefore, she decided to bless him.

At night, *Liandoia* could not sleep thinking about the next morning and what he would offer to his guest. On the other hand, the old woman was also eager to bless *Liandoia*. She quietly got up and fetched an empty paddy basket and began her magic power by pinching her nail with a porcupine quill. By doing so, the small sound of '*krit...krit...krit...*' came out followed by the sound of '*drill...drill...drill...*' Which in fact was the sound of

---

35 Ramdina Lalsim, *Tribes...,* 66.

36 Narendra S. Bisht, T. S. Bankoti, eds., *Encyclopaedic Ethnography of the Himalayan Tribes: A-D, Volume 1* (Delhi: Global Vision Pub House, 2004), 181.

37 Ramdina Lalsim, *Tribes...*, 103-105.

the grains of paddy falling into the basket? *Liandoia* heard the sound and asked the old woman what she was doing. The woman replied, "Kind man, I bless you, God bless you" as she continued her work. In no time, the entire baskets were full of paddy grains and even his *Pangh* (100 Qtl. capacity basket) became full with paddy overnight. *Liandoia* could not believe his eyes as his hut became full of grains and he was overjoyed. The old woman told him not to worry for grains in future and also promised to help him whenever he called for help during the harvesting time. She also advised him not to put an empty basket on a tree stump in an upside down position and not to whistle during the harvesting, if he did so all of a sudden the crops would decrease and get spoilt. In time, the kind and generous *Liandoia* called upon the *Fapite* every harvesting season and thus the poorest of the poor *Liandoia* became the richest in the entire village.

6. Significance of the Myth for Socio-Religious Transformation

The Biate myth that has been narrated in the previous section shows much similarity with the Mizo myth of *Liandova* and his brother *Tuaisiala*. However, there are certain differences as well. According to Ramdina Lalsim, there are two versions that have the same protagonist *Liandoia*. The other one also mentions his brother *Tuaisiala*.[38] Nevertheless, this particular myth of the Biates plays a significant role in enlightening us about the rich tribal heritage of the Biates and brings to light the immense socio-religious significance of tribal myths for the present day. These various significances may be enumerated as follows:

The old woman in the myth said to *Liandoia*, "Kind man, I bless you, God bless you." This shows that the old woman was a kind of lesser god or goddess and that the Biates believed in the existence of a Supreme Being who blessed the people. This belief is affirmed by Ramdina Lalsim who writes that, the Biates believed in the existence of a Supreme Being known as '*Chung*

[38] Personal telephone conversation with Mr. Ramdina Lalsim on 30 July 2013.

Pathian' which means 'Heavenly Holy Father.' Who is believed to be Omnipresent, is all in all, the beginning and the end of everything. The above narrated myth throws light on the diversity of the tribal religious pantheon. It shows that the tribals along with their belief in the existence of benevolent and malevolent spirits had a deep faith in the existence of an Eternal, Omnipresent and Omniscient Supreme Being who is the ground of all creation, who watches and sees everything and bestows blessings upon the deserving people.

The tribal concept of Supreme Being entails judgment and retribution, punishment and reward according to the deeds done on this earth. Therefore, the tribals strove hard to live an honest and upright life for fear of judgment and punishment in the afterlife as well as in this earthly existence. This concept demanded of the tribals to maintain a high standard of morality in this life in order to be rewarded in the afterlife. Hence, the tribal concept of the Supreme Being demands of us to uphold a high standard of morality and gives eschatological hope to the righteous and the just.

The myth also throws light on a socio-religious custom of the Biates. Since the *Fapite* advised *Liandoia* not to whistle during the harvesting, it is taboo for the Biates to whistle during the harvesting time. Moreover, from that time onwards, the Biates remember *Fapite* as the queen or grandmother of the paddy who once showed her miraculous power to the kind *Liandoia* and have appeased her in every ritual ceremony of the harvest.[39]

Taboo is a sacred interdict that takes into account the power that surrounds certain objects and activities. Although, all types of taboos may not come under the purview of sacred. However, taboo plays an important role in the social cohesion of the people. On the other hand, while people might be filled with fear at the thought of divine retribution if taboos are broken, they serve as a positive purpose for focusing one's life on the divine and the

---

[39] Ramdina Lalsim, *Tribes*..., 105.

purposes of the divine. Thus, one's life gets integrated with the divine.[40]

The myth also has ethical values as it teaches a valuable lesson regarding selfless service and hospitality to strangers and guests, which is a quality held in high regard among the tribals. *Liandoia* had only a small quantity of rice which he happily offered to the old woman without any thought of what he would eat the next morning. And as asserted by Prof. T. Vanlaltlani, such selfless acts are secretly marked by someone who wants to praise the name of the selfless person on one day or another.[41] Thus, *Liandoia* was rewarded by *Fapite* for his selfless service and hospitality.

Many of the tribal myths including the present one exhibit the awareness of the existence of a Supreme Being who watches over human beings irrespective of caste, gender, class or colour. These tales relate the good result of helping the needy and of generous service to the needy. They teach us the virtue of suffering on behalf of somebody else, sacrificing time and energy for the benefit of others and extending hospitality and charity to others, without the expectation of any reward whatsoever.

The teachings imbibed in these myths have become the kernel of tribal social and ethical life and moralistic attitude towards others. In today's world of individualism and consumerism, such selfless and moralistic attitudes as imparted by the tribal myths need to be rediscovered for a truly just and egalitarian society.

Another point of interaction with socio-moral attitudes from this myth relates to showing partiality towards people basing one's judgment on their outward appearances. None of the villagers could recognize that the old woman was in fact the rich and famous Queen of *Siset*. However, beneath the old woman lay the Queen in all her glory. Therefore, this myth teaches a valuable lesson that judging people from their physical appearance without knowing

[40] Sashikaba Kechutzar, "Rethinking Naga Religious Traditions: An Exploration of Tribal Christian Spirituality," in *Theologizing Tribal Heritage – A Critical Re-Look*, edited by Hrangthan Chhungi (Delhi: CWM/ISET-ECC/PCI/ISPCK, 2008), 181.

[41] T. Vanlaltlani, *Tribal Religion...*, 215.

their inner quality could misguide people in their interaction with other people in the society.

Furthermore, *Fapite*, is the queen of the paddy and she manifested herself in the form of an old woman. It was *Fapite* who became the source of blessing for the poor *Liandoia*. Moreover, she promised to help anytime *Liandoia* called upon her. Even though *Chung Pathian* was there, it was a female deity *Fapite* who shared in the suffering of *Liandoia* and who played an instrumental part in the economic liberation of the poor *Liandoia*. Therefore, this myth shows how important a part a woman can play in helping and liberating a person from the clutches of poverty and social impoverishment. This myth shows the caring, gentle and loving nature of women-folk who can become liberative agents in a male-dominated society.

Group solidarity is reinforced by reawakening the essence of identity by ritual narration of myths. Feeling of continuity is an experience of identity. Myths and rituals sponsor such a feeling. They are the expressions of an identity consciousness.[42] Thus, we can say that the myth mentioned provides a feeling of continuity with the foreparents and an experience of identity as a unique people with a glorious past.

This myth seems to have originated while the Biates were in Champhai valley, with its huge paddy fields.[43] Therefore, this myth also has a historical significance for the Biate community. It throws light on the past dwellings of the foreparents of the Biates as well.

Conclusion

The so-called tribal/primal people are often looked down upon by the non-tribals and professed civilized or developed people. But, the tribal culture and religion has rich elements that can enhance humanity as a whole. The tribal worldview and religion

---

[42] Sarthak Sengupta, ed., *Tribal Studies in North East India* (New Delhi: Mittal Publication, 2002), 37.

[43] Personal telephone conversation with Mr. Ramdina Lalsim on 30 July 2013.

with its land-centeredness and respect for all creation is valuable through the eyes of the ecological requirements of today. The global inclusive tribal worldview of challenges each and every human being to critically examine our concern and awareness for the creation and the natural resources for maintaining ecological balance.

Furthermore, myths are the ground of religion and contain the religious truth of a particular community. Myth teaches how the Supreme Being works and reveals the Godhead through creation, the place of human, and the animal kingdom in this universe, their relationship and so on.[44] The colorful myths and folklores of the tribals challenges humanity to go beyond the non-human world, beyond logical wisdom and aim to provide a holistic dimension, relatedness and interdependence of all creation.

[44] Longchar, *Myth...*, 83.

Chapter 3

Celebrating Hindu Festivals
Life's Valuable Lessons for Christians

The very term Hinduism is indeed very broad and vague. It describes an implausible variety of expression. As a result, David C. Scott has aptly remarked, "it has reasonably been suggested that it is not possible to characterize it as a religion in the normal sense since it is not a unitary concept nor a monolithic structure, but that it is rather a total way of life."[45] In studying the Hindu tradition, the absolute mass of different rituals and practices makes it impossible to endeavor a detailed study of the tradition. Our priority should be discerning the distinctive traits of the tradition, and what sets it apart from other religious traditions of the world.

However, in a religious tradition that is without a common doctrine, a hierarchy of authority or a historical founder, its distinctiveness is comprehendible only in terms of its history. Therefore, in approaching the Hindu tradition we have to rely

---

[45] David C. Scott, *The Hindu Religious Tradition*, in *Religious Traditions of India*, edited by P. S. Daniel, David C. Scott and G. R. Singh. (New Delhi: ISPCK, 1988), 75. Hereafter cited as Scott, *Hindu Religious...*

upon the historical and chronological events to sort out the shifting strands and patterns of collected tradition.[46]

1. Etymological Meaning and Definition of Hinduism

What makes Hinduism so hard to describe or define is not only its indistinguishable aspect, but also its variety, and its fluidity. It is not a static system, but a developing organism, full of movement. Mahatma Gandhi tried, albeit unsuccessfully, to give a definition of Hinduism in the following words:

> If I were asked, I should simply say: It is the search for truth through non-violent means. A man may not believe in God, and still call himself a Hindu. Hinduism is a relentless pursuit after truth. It is the religion of truth. Truth is God. Denial of God we have known. Denial of truth we have not known.[47]

Etymologically speaking, the actual term 'hindu' first occurs as a Persian geographical term to refer to the people who lived beyond the river Indus (Sanskrit: *sindhu*).[48] In Arabic texts, *Al-Hind* is a term for the people of modern-day India[49] and 'Hindu.' or 'Hindoo', was used towards the end of the 18th century by the British to refer to the people of 'Hindustan,' the area of northwest India. Eventually 'Hindu' became virtually equivalent to an 'Indian' who was not a Muslim, Sikh, Jain or Christian, thereby encompassing a range of religious beliefs and practices. The '-ism' was added to 'Hindu' in around 1830 to denote the culture and religion of the high-caste Brahmans in contrast to other religions, and the term was soon appropriated by Indians themselves in the context of establishing a national identity opposed to colonialism, though the term 'Hindu' was used in Sanskrit and Bengali

---

[46] Scott, *Hindu Religious...,* 75.

[47] A. C. Bouquet, *Hinduism* (London: Hutchinson and Co (Publishers) Ltd., 1949), 15,16.

[48] Gavin Flood, *An Introduction to Hinduism* (New Delhi: Cambridge University Press, 2004), 6. Hereafter cited as Flood, *Introduction to Hinduism...*

[49] Romila Thapar, *Interpreting Early India* (Delhi: Oxford University Press, 1993), 77.

hagiographic text in contrast to '*Yavana*' or Muslim, as early as the 16th century.[50]

Even though the Western world understands Hinduism simply as one of the major religions in the world, for Hindus it is much more than that: it is a way of life, a large and rich culture, an environment that envelops a Hindu from before birth to after death. What the so called Hinduism, Hindus themselves designate as *sanatana dharma*, 'eternal law,' that is identical with universally valid and generally binding insights and precepts, specified so as to accord with the individuals' standing within society.[51] Within the framework of *sanatana dharma* a great many different *sampradayas*, religious communities with specific beliefs, rituals and places of worship, flourish.[52]

2. Major Hindu Festivals

Every religion sets aside certain days as days of rejoicing as well as of worship and prayer. These days we celebrate birthdays and other significant events in the lives of the great personalities of a religion or in celebration of some special occasion or in observance of some cherished ideal. The followers of Hinduism also gave a number of festive days that are observed with great joy and passion.

Hindu festivals surprise the foreigner by their obvious frequency and irregularity. But, the Hindu festivals have their own regularity and consistency, based on the movements of the heavenly bodies. Thus, there is more regularity underlying Hindu festivals than strangers may realize.[53] Thus, an attempt will be made to describe some major Hindu festivals and try to understand the rationale behind the celebration of these festivals and also try

---

[50] Flood, *Introduction to Hinduism...*, 6.

[51] Klaus K. Klostermaier, *Hinduism: A Short Introduction* (Oxford: Oneworld Publications, 2006), 2. Herafter cited as Klostermaier, *Hinduism...*

[52] Klostermaier, *Hinduism...*, 2.

[53] Henry H. Presler, *Introducing strangers to Hinduism* (Allahabad: North India Christian Tract & Book Society, 1978), 235-236.

to draw some relevant lessons Christians can learn from the Hindu way of festive celebrations.

There are numerous festivals as well as feasts and auspicious days in the Hindu faith. A number of these festivals are common to most parts of India. However, they may be called by various names in various parts of the country or may be celebrated in various fashions. Moreover, each and every festival is not celebrated by all sections of the society. But, so vast is the number of feasts and festivals that Klostermaier has remarked, "Apart from the more or less universal ones, there are countless local feasts; catalogues count more than a thousand—enough to demonstrate that no Hindu can practice all of Hinduism."[54]

For the sake of convenience, we will confine ourselves to the major Hindu festivals as put forwarded by P. L. Bhargava who has described them in a chronological order:

a) *Holi*: *Holi* is celebrated on the first day of the month of *Caitra* (March-April) which is the first month of the Hindu year. Bhargava says that, this festival is also observed to commemorate the beginning of spring or *vasanta*, therefore it is also called *Vasantotsva* or the Spring festival. Furthermore, he says that, the word Holi (Sanskrit *holaka*, Hindi *hola*) which means 'chick pea or pulse half parched in the pod,' is also significant. At the time of the new harvest, people joyfully parch sheaves of grain and eat it. Hence this festival has come to be called Holi.[55]

The legends connected with *Holi* are the legend in *Vaishnava* theology about *Hiranyakashipu*, the king of demons and his son *Prahlada* who was miraculously saved by Vishnu from the sacrificial fire that was meant to burn him to death, the legend of the demoness *Holika* who used to devour one child a day and who was killed by a volley of filthy abuse from children. In Bengal,

---

[54] Klaus K. Klostermaier, *A Survey of Hinduism* (United States of America: State University of New York Press, 2007), 280. Hereafter cited as Klostermaier, *Survey*...

[55] P. L. Bhargava, *Fundamentals of Hinduism: A Rational Analysis* (New Delhi: Munshiram Manoharlal Publishers Pvt. Ltd., 1982), 84. Hereafter cited as Bhargava, *Fundamentals*...

where the festival is known as *Doljatra*, it evokes *Krsna's* amours with the *gopis*. *Krsna* is said to have complained to his mother about the contrast between his dark colour and his consort *Radha's* fair colour. *Krsna's* mother decided to apply colour to *Radha's* face. In South India, it commemorates the burning out of *Kama*, the god of love by Siva who was tempted by *Kama* while he was in the middle of his meditation.

Holi is celebrated for two days and on the first day, huge bonfires depicting the demoness *Holika* is burnt and on the second day, known as *Dhulhendi*, people spend the day throwing coloured powder and water at each other. The spring season, during which the weather changes, is believed to bring with it viral fever and cold. Therefore, the playful throwing of coloured powders made from *Neem*, *Kumkum*, *Haldi*, *Bilva* and other medicinal herbs prescribed by Ayurvedic doctors, is believed to have medicinal significance. A special drink called *thandai* (prepared from bhang or Cannabis sativa) is prepared and drunk. *Rangapanchami* occurs a few days later on a *Panchami* (5th day of the full moon), thus the festivities involving colours come to an end.[56]

b) *Ramanavami*: *Ramanavami* is the celebration of the birth anniversary of Rama, the Ideal Man. It falls on the ninth day of the bright fortnight of the month of *Caitra* (March-April).[57] Rama is the Incarnation of Vishnu who took his birth at his own will in order to establish righteousness, destroy the wicked and protect his devotees.[58] On this day the devout Hindus observe a fast till midday and read portions relating to the birth of Ramayana from the Ramayana. At midday people congregate to Rama temples and participate in the worship of Rama. The celebrations conclude with the devotees partaking of the *prasada* (food and drink sanctified by being offered to the Lord).[59]

---

[56] Rajeev Verma, *Faith and Philosophy of Hinduism* (Delhi: Kalpaz Publications, 2009), 255. Hereafter cited as Verma, *Faith and Philosophy...*

[57] Bhargava, *Fundamentals...*, 84.

[58] Verma, *Faith and Philosophy...*, 256.

[59] Bhargava, *Fundamentals...*, 84.

c) *Raksabandhana*: This festival comes more than four months after *Ramanavami* when the rainy season is in full swing, on the full moon day of the month of *Sravana* (July August). On this day girls tie colored threads round their brothers' wrists and make them their protectors, receiving a small gift in return. According to a legend *Indra* was saved from the demon *Bali* through the magical armlet that his wife had tied for him.[60] A brotherless woman may also make a man her brother by tying a rakhi on his wrist or sending him one. This festival is in observance of a cherished ideal of Hindu society, the sister's concern for her brother's welfare. So far as the ritual aspect of this festival is concerned, it is a day dedicated to learning, when the orthodox put on the sacred thread anew and worship *Sarasvati*, the goddess of learning.[61]

d) *Krsna Janmastami*: *Krsna Janmastami* is the celebration of the birth anniversary of *Krsna*, the apostle of the *Bhagavadgita*. It falls on the eight day of the dark fortnight of *Bhadrapada* (August-September).[62] From the beginning of the dark fortnight the god's praises are sung at musical recitals. After the seventh day, at midnight, a special worship is held. In many houses a room is set apart to represent the prison where *Krsna* was born and the stable where he was transferred, with colourful images of the god, his mother *Devaki*, his murderous uncle *Kamsa*, etc. Dishes of sweets are presented to the child-god, and then eaten by the inmates of the house. In Bengal, the religious rites are accompanied by processions of singing and dancing devotees.[63]

e) *Vijaya Dasami/Dasara*: *Vijaya Dasami* is the festival of victory and is popularly known as *Dasara*. It falls on the tenth day of the bright fortnight of *Asvina* (September-October) when the skies become clear with the advent of autumn. This festival

---

[60] Klostermaier, *Survey...,* 280.

[61] Bhargava, *Fundamentals...*, 85.

[62] Bhargava, *Fundamentals...*, 85.

[63] A. Huart, "Hindu Calendar and Festivals," in *Religious Hinduism: A Presentation and Appraisal,* edited by R. De Smet and J. Neuner (Mumbai: St. Pauls, 1964), 138. Hereafter cited as Huart, *Hindu Calendar...*

is observed in celebration of the victory of *Rama* over *Ravana*, which symbolizes the victory of good over evil. From the beginning of this fortnight, popular plays portraying the exploits of *Rama* known as *Ramalilas* are staged in the evenings in every city and village and people gather in large numbers to watch them. These plays conclude on the *Dasara* day with the display of fireworks and the burning of the effigies of Ravana and his brother *Kumbhakarna* and son *Meghanada*.[64]

f) *Diwali*: *Dipotsava* or *Dipavali*, the festival of lights, popularly known as *Diwali* is the greatest and grandest of Hindu festivals. It falls on the new moon day of *Kartika* (October-November), when the weather is perfect. On this day, people purchase sweets and on *Diwali* evening the houses and shops are all illuminated with earthen lamps or electric bulbs as per the convenience of the owners. Besides illuminations, there is also display of fireworks which begins a few days before *Diwali*. On the next day people visit their friends and relatives to offer their good wishes. In the afternoon, the devout prepare a heap of boiled rice, with curry and other delicacies and invite their friends to partake of these dishes. The third and concluding day of *Diwali* is called *Bhratr Dvitiya* or the Brothers' Day. On this day sisters invite their brothers to a feast and the brothers give some gifts to them in return.[65]

With regards to the origin of this festival, according to a widely prevalent tradition in Northern India, it is the homecoming of King *Rama* after his 14-year exile in the forest. The people of Ayodhya welcomed *Rama* by lighting rows of lamps, thus its name *Dipavali*, or *Diwali*. Southern India, on the other hand marks it as the day when *Krsna* defeated the demon *Narakasura*. In Western India it is also in honor of the day King *Bali* went to rule the netherworld by the order of *Vishnu*. As per one theory, *Diwali* may have started as a harvest festival, marking the last harvest of the year before the onset of winter. In an agrarian society this results in businessmen closing accounts, and beginning a new accounting

---

[64] Bhargava, *Fundamentals...*, 85-86.

[65] Bhargava, *Fundamentals...*, 86.

year. The deity of wealth, goddess *Lakshmi* is thus thanked on this day and all pray for a good year to come. This is one common factor in the celebration of *Diwali* throughout India.[66]

Diwali marks the victory of good over evil, and overcoming of spiritual darkness. Symbolically, it marks the homecoming of goodwill and faith after an absence, as suggested by the *Ramayana*. The most significant spiritual meaning is 'the awareness of the inner light.' Hindu philosophy asserts the existence of the *Atman* which is pure, infinite, and eternal. Just as the birth of the physical being is celebrated, *Diwali* is the celebration of this Inner Light, in particular, the realization of *Atman*, or awakening of one's true nature which brings universal compassion, love, and the awareness of the oneness of all things. This brings *Ananda* (Inner Joy or Peace).[67]

Besides the festivals described above, there are numerous others such as, *Guru Purnima, Sankranti, Vasanta Panchami, Ganesh Chaturthi, Hanuman Jayanti, Shivaratri, Onam* etc. But, many of these festivals are celebrated by certain sects or by people living in a particular region only. The major festivals described above are celebrated by the majority of Hindus living worldwide and they occupy an important place in the life of every Hindu.

3. Rationale Behind the Celebration of Festivals

It can be seen that there is a huge amount of mythological data involved in the festivals. But, few take seriously the involved mythology behind the festivals. At the same time many regard such observances as auspicious and expressive of a deep religious truth.

Besides the mythological reasons for the celebration of these festivals, the festivals are intended to serve as occasions for intensive contemplation of god. They are supposed to be holidays from worldly life and opportune occasions for a person to search his/her heart. From the description given above, we have seen that almost all the festivals commemorates the glory of god

[66] Verma, *Faith and Philosophy...,* 253-254.

[67] Verma, *Faith and Philosophy...,* 254-255.

which vanquishes evil and enables good to triumph. Therefore, symbolically, these festivals mean the overcoming of all that is evil in us by the higher or real self.

Many festivals are purification fasts. The followers of each cult have their own particular days in the year which they spend solely in prayer and worship. Many people on these occasions fast and keep vigil during the night, read from the sacred texts and keep their minds engaged in contemplation on god. There are also days on which women fast and offer prayer to the goddess in her various manifestations. These fasts are named *vratas* or vows.[68] These fasts are intended for the purification of the soul and providing it with spiritual food.

The one purpose underlying all the festivals is the creation of a spiritual climate for the people, an atmosphere in which they can find their spiritual health and nurture their souls. These festivals are days of renewal of contact with god. The spiritual people do not make any difference between sacred and secular days; every day is a holy day for them. But, all people are not so spiritually conscious, therefore, they have a long way ahead in their spiritual journey. Therefore, they need special days of prayer and religious rest. The festivals serve this spiritual purpose and are times which make the Hindus commune with god.[69]

There is also a social dimension to the celebration of festivals. Hindu religiosity and spirituality is basically an individual affair, a matter of private meditation or at the most a family *puja*. Thus, the celebration of festivals is a social affair. Since they are a mixture of mythology and folklore, worship and celebration, magic and seasonal customs, astrology and local traditions, they introduce into the religious life of the Hindu a certain measure of communal worship and communication with the divine as a believing community. They are occasions of genuine prayer and joy.[70]

---

[68] T. M. P. Mahadevan, *Outlines of Hinduism* (Bombay: Chetana Pvt. Ltd., 1954), 50-51. Hereafter cited as Mahadevan, *Outlines...*

[69] Mahadevan, *Outlines...*, 52.

[70] Huart, *Hindu Calendar...,* 143.

4. Relevant Life Lessons to be Learnt by Christians

In many Hindu feasts and festivals, it is common to find obscene and immoral behaviors and activities. But in spite of these, Hindu festivals have many lessons to offer to Christians. Let us contemplate upon the lessons that we can learn from the Hindu celebration of their festivals as follows:

a) During the time of festivals, Hindu women put on all their jewellery and finest clothes to worship god. The temples and houses are also decorated. But, the lesson to be learnt is as asserted by Nirad C. Chaudhuri, Yet in all this display there was no motive of showing off, present or perceived. Here at all events the extravagant Hindu adornments became a part of devotion, as if it was only an offering to the gods."[71]

In the celebration of Christmas by Christians, it is highly doubtful whether all the decorations and the new clothes are meant to be a part of devotion or as an offering to God. Outward preparations have become so extreme that Christmas, a time of joy has become a time of depression for many families. Christians should remember the teaching of the Bible, "Do not adorn yourselves outwardly by braiding your hair, and by wearing gold ornaments or fine clothing; rather, let your adornment be the inner self with the lasting beauty of a gentle and quiet spirit, which is very precious in God's sight." (1 Pet. 3:3)

b) Two festivals, viz. *Raksabandhana* and *Bhratr Dvitiya*, the third and final day of the *Diwali* festival are celebrations of the love between a brother and a sister. As has been mentioned even a brotherless woman can make a man her brother by tying a *rakhi* or by sending one. Such festivals are symbolical of the brotherliness/sisterliness that should characterize the relation of one human to another.

Such festivals of the celebration of love serve a valuable lesson not only to Christians but to all humanity in an age of violence against women and where love for our fellow human beings has become a rare commodity. We need to remember

[71] Nirad C. Chaudhuri, *Hinduism: A Religion to Live By* (New Delhi: B.I. Publications, 1979), 300.

afresh the teaching of the Bible, "Owe no one anything, except to love one another; for the one who loves another has fulfilled the law." (Rom. 13:8)

c) In Hindu festivals, people go visiting their friends, wishing them all happiness and freedom from all kinds of oppressive forces. The delicacies prepared on these festive occasions are shared with friends and relatives.

But in today's world, modern human beings are very busy persons, producing and consuming. Hospitality has become a rare virtue, and guests are seen as a nuisance.[72] From the hospitality shown to guests on the occasion of the festivals, Christians should remember the teaching of the Bible, "Do not neglect to show hospitality to strangers, for by doing that some have entertained angels without knowing it." (Heb. 13:2)

d) The brotherliness/sisterliness that should characterize the relation of humans among themselves ought to extend to mute creation also. Part of *Diwali* celebrations is the worship of animals, especially cows. They are not seen merely from the utility point of view, but as members of the family.[73] Mahatma Gandhi has this to say about showing concern to the cow:

> Cow protection to me is infinitely more than mere protection of the cow. The cow is merely a type for all that lives. Cow protection means protection of the weak, the helpless, the dumb and the deaf. Man becomes then not the lord and master of all creation but he is its servant.[74]

Christianity that has often been criticized for its other worldliness and as being the cause for the ecological crisis faced by the world today should realize that, the dominion over all creation granted to human beings by God does not grant us the right to

---

72 Subhash Anand, *Major Hindu Festivals: A Christian Appreciation* (Bombay: St. Paul Publications, 1991), 123. Hereafter cited as Anand, *Major Hindu Festivals*...

73 Anand, *Major Hindu Festivals...*, 123.

74 V. B. Kher, ed., *In Search of the Supreme,* 3 vols. (Ahmedabad: Navajivan Publishing House, 1962), 202, cited by Anand, *Major Hindu Festivals...*, 124.

misuse the creation for our selfish gains. In fact, Christians need to realize that the command is not domination but stewardship (Gen. 1:28).

e) The Church in India has often been criticized because of its Western leanings and conversion to Christianity is seen by many Hindus as abandoning one's culture and traditions. But, it should be noted that whenever it was possible, the Church has assimilated to its own liturgy the religious festivals which persons were accustomed to keep before they knew anything about Christ.[75]

The Church in India would also do well to adopt some of the festivals which are dear to Indians such as, *Raksabandhana* as the feast of brotherly love, *Diwali*, as the feast of Christ, the Light of the World etc. Of course, it must be done with a certain amount of transformation, but it can retain the core of their meaning through which human beings can raise their heart to the true God.

Conclusion

Thus, from the above discussion, we can conclude by saying that the number of festivals in Hinduism is so numerous that it is difficult even for Hindus to celebrate and observe all of them. But, as has been mentioned, not all festivals are celebrated by all Hindus. Many festivals are regional festivals celebrated by people of a particular region only. Hindu festivals as has been seen are a mixture of mythology, magic and superstition accompanied by immense crowds, wildness and complete absence of reverence and self-restraint, and consequently Christian missionaries in the past had denounced them as grossly immoral. But, as has been pointed out, these Hindu festivals have many lessons to be learnt from them that can enrich Christianity and humanity as a whole.

[75] Huart, *Hindu Calendar...*, 144.

Chapter 4

Call to Eco-Jihad
Islam and an Eco-Just Society

The ecological crisis is one of the most important issues facing humanity today. Ecological degradation due to ruthless and wanton exploitation of nature has created a chain of inter-related problems that has adversely affected human beings and other living things.

All religions of the world confess God's presence in the cosmos, and no religion preaches use of violence against nature. All religions attribute, in varying degrees, sacredness to water, fire, mountains, rivers, trees etc. and use them symbolically in their religious worship and are mentioned in their sacred scriptures as objects dear to God and sacred to the faithful.[76] Therefore, we can say that religion has an important role to play in addressing the ecological crisis that is being faced by the world today.

In 1967, the historian Lynn White Junior propounded a controversial theory regarding the origins of the ecological crisis,

---

[76] Augustine Thottakara, "Introduction," in *Eco-Spirituality – Perspectives from World Religions*, edited by Augustine Thottakara (Rome: Centre for Indian and Inter-Religious Studies, 1995), vii-viii.

namely that its roots lay in monotheistic religions. Reactions to this accusation from the religious quarter triggered a new discourse of 'ecotheology.' Although, White focused primarily on Christianity and Judaism in his writings, the confrontation with such an allegation and the perception of the ecological crisis led Muslims to turn their attention to the issue of ecology as well.[77]

Islam is probably one of the most criticized religions today because of Islamic fundamentalism and global terror perpetrated by these fundamentalists. However, like other religious traditions, Islam also has heartfelt concerns for an eco-just society. As Max Muller so emphatically remarked, "*To know one is to know none.*" Hence, to know the religious teaching of just one religion is inadequate in order to discern to liberative motifs present in other religious traditions. Therefore, attempt has been made to identify the teachings of Islam concerning nature and creation and draw out its concern for the ecology and the responsibility of humankind towards nature for an eco-just society.

1. Islam: A Brief Overview

On the basis of population, after Christianity, Islam, the religion founded by Prophet Muhammad is the second largest religious movement in the world. It is estimated that there are over 50 crores Islamic adherents in the world today. About 620 lakhs of Muslims are there in India.[78] Islam is the youngest of the three monotheistic world religions, with Muhammad coming after the prophets of Judaism and Christianity.[79]

Muhammad, the founder of Islam was born in the "Year of the Elephant" (about the early 570s) to 'Abd Allah of the

---

[77] http://environment-ecology.com/religion-and-ecology.html (29 July, 2017).

[78] Geevarghese Yulios, *Message of Religions: Doing Theology with Asian Religious Resources* (Kolkata: PTCA/SCEPTRE, 2013), 175. Hereafter cited as Yulios, *Message of Religions: Doing Theology with Asian Religious Resources* (Kolkata: PTCA/SCEPTRE, 2013), 175.

[79] Gordon D. Newby, *A Concise Encyclopedia of Islam* (Oxford, England: Oneworld Publications, 2002), 3.

Hashimite clan of the Quraysh and Amina of the clan of Zuhra. His father died four months before he was born and his mother also died a few years later. As was the custom, he was raised by a Bedouin nurse, Halima, and then stayed with his grandfather 'Abd al-Muttalib and later with his uncle Abu Talib. At age 25, Muhammad married Khadijah, a wealthy woman of about 40 for whom he had conducted business.[80]

Arabia, the birthplace of Islam during the 6th century A.D. was a desert region where a large number of clans who were often engaged in quarrels and inter-clan feuds lived together. Even though in principle all of them had the concept of a single god who was the creator of the universe, Allah, each clan had its own god-goddesses concepts and ways of worship. They were not unified as a nation and there was no unified administration. However, most of the clans believed that they were the descendents of Ismael who was the son of Ibrahim Nabi (Abraham).[81]

Muhammad, was a deeply religious person and every year in the month of Rajab, he would go to Mount Hira and live there and spend his time in spiritual contemplation and fasting. When he was 40 years of age, he came home one day, confessing to Khadija that he heard voices. And one day in the month of Ramadan, Muhammad had his first revelation. This was followed by other revelations, and an angel later identified as Gabriel told Muhammad that he was chosen as the Messenger of God.[82] Soon Muhammad had a small band of followers and he began to propagate his message of the one true God, Allah.

Islam is often seen as having the simplest doctrines of the major religions. The most fundamental concept of Islam is a rigorous monotheism, called *tawḥīd.* Islam rejects polytheism and idolatry, called *Shirk.* In Islam, God is beyond all comprehension and thus Muslims are not expected to think of him as having a human form. The Muslims believe that the *Qur'an,* the Holy

---

[80] Ludwig W. Adamec, *The A-to-Z of Islam* (New Delhi: Vision Books Pvt. Ltd., 2003), 2. Hereafter cited as Adamec, *A-to-Z...*

[81] Yulios, *Message of Religions...,* 175.

[82] Adamec, *A-to-Z...,* 2-3.

Scripture of Islam is the eternal word of god, written for eternity on the plaque called *Louh ulmah fooz* and kept near the throne of god in heaven. It is believed to have been brought down and given to Muhammad by the Angel Gabriel in the month of Ramadan for the salvation of the world.

The entire Islamic theology can be summarized in the short creed *La ilaha-illallah, Muhammadur Rasullullah* which simply means, Allah is One and Muhammad is his *Rasul* (Prophet). This short confession of faith is considered so important that it is whispered into the ears of a new-born child and every attempt is made to make these the last words of a dying person.[83] Besides the doctrine of God, Islamic theology is based on 5 other doctrinal beliefs such as Belief in Angels, Belief in Scripture, Belief in Prophets, Belief in the Resurrection and Final Judgement and Belief in Predestination. These 6 doctrinal beliefs are together known as the 'Pillars of Islam.'

Islam is broadly divided into *iman* (faith) and *din* (faith in action). Just as there are 6 articles of faith, there are 5 fundamental duties of every Muslim which are known as *arkanu'd din*. These 5 duties are *Tashahud/Shahada, Salat* (daily prayers), *Saum/Roza* (fasting during the month of *Ramadan*), *Zakat/Sadaqa* (Giving of Offerings) and *Hajj* (Pilgrimage to Mecca).[84]

Muhammad died at Medina in 632 A.D. But, by then he was able to bring Arabia religiously and politically under the banner of Islam. Muhammad's followers, who continued the tradition and teachings of Muhammad developed Arabia into an unconquerable power and at the same time elevated Islam, to a position of a known world-religion.[85] At the birth of Muhammad, there was nothing to indicate that the militaristic tribes of Arabia, united only occasionally in the interests of trade and religion, would become one mighty people conquering their powerful neighbours. But, it can be rightly said that it was Islam that transformed these

[83] Lalchawiliana Varte, *Islam Sakhua Hi Eng Nge?* (Aizawl: Sangthuami, 2019), 67. Hereafter cited as Lalchawiliana, *Islam Sakhua...*

[84] Lalchawiliana, *Islam Sakhua...*, 83-95.

[85] Yulios, *Message of Religions...*, 176-177.

merchant nomads into a great religious, cultural and juridico-political entity that swept and encompassed the world.

2. Etymological Meaning of Ecology

The term 'ecology' has been derived from the Greek word '*oikos*,' which means 'house.' The term originally referred to a branch of biology and it is still used in this sense. The term was coined by the German biologist Ernst Haeckel in 1866, to designate the newly developing "science of habitat." It refers to that branch of biology which investigates the relations of the living beings among one another and to their particular place, its climate, character of the soil, etc.[86]

The American Ecologist, E. A. Gutkind, used this term in 1954. It describes saying that within the green movement which sees the present ecological crisis as a result of the breakdown of the organic fabric of both society and nature. It is concerned with the green movement with democracy, community and co-operation. It has a realization that there exist social and political institutions of dominations and hierarchy that block the liberation of nature and humanity.[87]

3. Islam and Creation

The word earth (*ard*) is mentioned 485 times in the *Qur'an*. *Shari'ah*, the word usually translated to mean "Islamic law" also literally means "source of water." The *Shari'ah* is the source of life in that it contains both ethical and legal rules.[88] According to the *Qur'an*, the world and whatever God decided to create in it came into existence by His sheer command: "Be" (2:117; 3:47, 59; 6:73 etc.). God is, therefore, the absolute possessor of the universe and its unquestioned commander, just as He is its merciful sustainer.

---

[86] Karl H. Peschke, *Christian Ethics Moral Theology in the Light of Vatican II* (Bangalore: Theological Publications in India, 1996), 756.

[87] R. L. Sarkar, *The Bible, Ecology and Environment* (Delhi: ISPCK/CISRS, 2000), 65-66.

[88] http://www.hollys7.tripod.com/religionandecology.html (01 September 2013).

Hence, the *Qur'an* considers the whole universe as "Muslim," because everything inside it (except human, who may or may not become "Muslim") has "surrendered itself to God's will" (3:83), and everything glorifies God (57:1; 59:1; 61:1 etc.).[89] Nature is the mirror of God's knowledge, might, wisdom and grace. By thinking about nature's majesty and splendor one can realize the omnipotence, grandeur and magnificence of its Creator; a mighty, wise and merciful God, who did not create the universe and humankind in vain.[90]

The *Qur'an* time and again cites that nature, so well knit and working with such regularity is the prime miracle of God. No being other than God could have built this vast and secure structure (67: 3-4; 27:88).[91] However, human beings deride or ignore or even rebel against God, because they consider the working of the natural processes as having some rational explanation. Humankind do not take the ordered universe to be a sign or a miracle, but look for miracles that are contradictory to the natural processes. Nature with its unimaginable vastness and regularity should serve as God's sign for humans, since none but an infinite and unique Being could have created it and this may be called a "natural sign," a kind of natural revelation of the existence of a Supreme Creator.

The mosque holds a pivotal position in Islam as the place where God is worshipped. Islam teaches that the *Qur'an*, the Prophet, or nature, are all reflections of the sacred texts of God. Humankind, nature and God are intrinsically related to each other through Islamic worship. Nature is the mosque par excellence captures the believer's relationship both to God and to nature

---

[89] Fazlur Rahman, *Major Themes of the Qur'an* (Chicago: The University of Chicago Press, 2009), 65. [Hereafter cited as Rahman, *Major Themes*...]

[90] Mohammed Masjed Jame'l, "The Monotheistic Vision of Man and Nature," in *Eco-Spirituality – Perspectives from World Religions,* edited by Augustine Thottakara (Rome: Centre for Indian and Inter-Religious Studies, 1995), vii-viii.

[91] Rahman, *Major Themes*..., 68.

as the creation of God.[92] Thus, we can say that according to the teachings of Islam, nature in all its beauty is a majestic mosque where God is to be worshipped and magnified.

According to the *Qur'an*, nature exists for humankind's purpose, while the purpose of humankind is to serve God and be grateful to Him, and to worship Him alone. Nature as the utility of humankind is spoken by the *Qur'an* in numerous verses (2: 29; 31:20; 45:12ff etc.). Even though all such verses portray God's power, their primary interest is to show God's use of His power for the betterment of human beings. Nevertheless, human beings are invited to use this opportunity for the good and not to "corrupt the earth."[93]

Thus, we can see that even though nature is intended to be of utility and sacrifice to humankind, nature and all creation is God's creation for the betterment of humankind. Nature is to be utilized for the good and betterment of humanity as a whole and humankind is charged with the responsibility of responsibly utilizing the resources of the earth and not to corrupt the earth. The *Qur'an* reiterates that the creation of the universe was a serious affair, not a sport or a triviality (38:27; cf. 3:191). Nature is the grand handiwork of God, but it does not exist just to show off His might and power. It is to serve humankind by providing the vital needs.[94] Thus, human being's purpose is to do good in this world, and not substitute themselves for God and think that they are able to make or break the moral law at their own convenience to satisfy their selfish or narrow greed.

4. Islam and Humankind

Humankind is God's creature just like any other created being. He is, indeed a natural creation, for God fashioned Adam out of baked clay (15:26, 28, 33; 6:2; 7:12, etc.). However, human beings are distinguished from the rest of the natural creation by the fact that

---

[92] Abdulkader Tayob, *Islam – A Short Introduction* (Oxford, England: Oneworld Publications, 2006), 81-82.

[93] Rahman, *Major Themes...*, 78-79.

[94] Rahman, *Major Themes...*, 79.

after fashioning humankind, God "breathed My own spirit" into human (15:29; 38:72; 32:9).[95] Human life is distinguished from the types of animal life by one single power which is called the power of reason, *nutq*.[96]

However, the Muslim scholar Akhlaq-i-Nasiri teaches that, in regard to what human has in common with animals and other forms of life, that if the animal nature prevails over human and their inclination are in that direction, they will be degraded from their proper rank to that of the order of beasts, or even lower. For the *Qur'an* says, "They are like the brutes. Yea, they go more astray" (7:178).[97]

Nevertheless, humankind has not been created in sport, but has a serious duty (23:115) and is answerable for his success or failure; for both God and humankind have taken a serious risk in this vital affair, i.e. the vice-regency of humankind.[98] To humankind is given the role of *khalifa* (trustee): "Behold, the Lord said to the angels: 'I will create a viceregent on earth. . . .'" (2:30). But, it is a role that each person must perform wisely and responsibly, fully aware of human accountability to the Almighty. "Do no mischief on the earth after it hath been set in order, but call on him with fear and longing in your hearts: for the Mercy of God is always near to those who do good (7:56). In other parts of the *Qur'an* we read that God rejoices in creation; all nature declares God's bounteousness; the variety in creation points to the unity in the divine plan; and God gave humankind spiritual insight so that it should understand nature. Moreover, the principle of balance is fundamental to that plan: "And the earth We have spread out like a carpet; set thereon mountains firm and immobile; and produced therein all kinds of things in due balance" (15:19).[99]

---

[95] Rahman, *Major Themes*..., 17.

[96] Dwight M. Donaldson, *Studies in Muslim Ethics* (London: SPCK, 1953), 172. Hereafter cited as Donaldson, *Studies*...

[97] Donaldson, *Studies...,* 171.

[98] Rahman, *Major Themes*..., 19.

[99] Marjorie Hope and James Young, "Islam and Ecology," http://www.crosscurrents.org/islamecology.htm (03 September 2013).

5. Relation Between Humankind and Creation in Islam

The *Qur'an* is replete with ethical teachings related to humankind's relation to the created universe. With regards to water, the *Qur'an* says "... and We made every living thing of water ..." (21:30). For water is the secret of life, and Islam forbids the wastage of water, and the usage thereof without benefit. The *Qur'an* further says "Have you observed the water which you drink? Is it you who shed it from the raincloud or are We the shedder." (56: 68&69). The preservation of water for the drinking of humankind, animal life, birdlife, and vegetation is a form of worship which gains the pleasure of Allah. Islam also forbade urinating in pools of still water, or otherwise contaminating water bodies.[100] From this the inference can be drawn that Islam also forbids sewerage and factory outpours to go to waterways, or to the ocean as this would pollute the water and threaten marine life.

There is abundant evidence to show that the ethic of universal love has been fully emphasized and is oriented in the *Qur'anic* tradition. In the *Qur'an*, there are many references to the unity of all being created by God. It says: "there is not an animal that lives on earth, not a being that flies on two wings but they are living beings like unto you." This shows that unity of all creations in the being of God is recognized in Islam.[101]

Prophet Mohammad (peace and blessings upon him) says that any Muslim who plants or cultivates vegetation and eats from it, or another person, animal or bird, eats from it will receive a reward for it from Allah. He (Peace and blessings upon him) also said that anyone who plants a tree under which people seek shade or shelter from the sun will have his reward with Allah. Therefore, the cutting down of trees without strong and legitimate reasons is

---

[100] "Islam and Ecology," http://www.speednet.com.au/~keysar/ecology.htm (02 September 2013).

[101] N. K. Singh, *Islam – A Religion of Peace* (Delhi: Global Vision Publishing House, 2002), 24. Hereafter cited as Singh, *Islam*...

encroachment on the bounties of Allah, and encroaching on the beauty of the environment which Allah has created.[102]

In Islam, the killing of an animal for food and for the good of humankind is not prohibited. However, the permission to kill does not mean an unmerciful behavior towards animals or other living creatures. Mercy and kindness towards all comprises the general ethic of Islam. Some of the cardinal elements in the Islamic system of values are emphasized on love for all, mercy and kindness to others, faith in unity of all humankind, and acceptance of the equality of all creatures in the kingdom of God.[103] The *Hadith* also forbids the eating of meat while on pilgrimage or holy war, and lays down rules against the killing of animals when they are in a helpless condition.[104]

Furthermore, According to Islamic teaching, air is the property of Allah the Exalted. If it was held from us for a few minutes, we would suffocate; it is also the means for communication as it carries sound between people. Hence, contaminating the air with smoke is an encroachment on nature, and a threat to the life of humankind and all other living things.[105]

6. Islam and an Eco-Just Society: The Call to Eco-Jihad

Thus, from the above discussion on the teaching of Islam on creation, human beings and the relation of human beings with creation, we can make out the following ecological concerns that Islam has, such as:

a) Islamic belief includes nature actively praising God in its continuous existence and movement. Although, the *Qu'ran* does state in certain cases that the environment is here to serve human, Islamic ecological ethics are derived from the belief that all of creation belongs to God, and not to humankind, and to assume

---

[102] "Islam and Ecology," http://www.speednet.com.au/~keysar/ecology.htm (02 September 2013).

[103] Singh, *Islam...*, 25.

[104] Singh, *Islam...*, 31.

[105] "Islam and Ecology," http://www.speednet.com.au/~keysar/ecology.htm (02 September 2013).

that animals and plants exist to benefit human beings leads to environmental destruction and misuse. If, as in Islamic belief, the component parts of nature are in continuous praise to God, human destruction of these parts prevents the earth's natural and subtle means for praising God. The *Qu'ran* acknowledges that humans are not the only creature to walk the earth.

b) Human is the most favoured of God's creation. Everything in existence was created by God for the use of humans. God has made subservient to humans all animal life, bird life, plant life, water bodies, inanimate objects, and other creations. Therefore, it is the duty of human beings to deal with these as a loving and caring friend would deal with another friend, so that they can benefit from creation, without stopping others from this benefit, and to put forward the common good ahead of personal benefit.

These created beings are partners to human in existence, and they deserve their own respect and have their own positions. They have been created for human beings, and without them, it would not be possible for human to survive. For, it is the vegetation that produces oxygen which humanity relies on for breathing. It is necessary for humankind to realize that Islam has placed restrictions and rules for the preservation of the environment, so that it can protect it from the behaviour, and the stupidity of some of the people, who treat it with ignorance and irresponsibility.

c) Islam considers the creation of the universe an open book, a guide inviting observation which increases the faith of the observer, and takes him to the point of unshakeable faith in the Great Creator of this existence. The created universe is God's 'miracle,' that silently preaches the omnipotence, omniscience, omnipresence of God through its natural processes. The *Qur'an* says, "*In the creation of the heavens and the earth, and the difference of night and day, and the ships which run upon the sea with that which is of use to people, and the water which Allah sends down from the sky, thereby reviving the earth after its death, and dispersing all kinds of beasts therein, and the ordinance of the winds, are signs for people who have sense*" (2:164).

d) The basic principle of all monotheistic religion, including Islam is God, not humankind. Both humankind and the universe were created by God and are subjected to His will. So, God is the Lord of humankind and nature. He provides for humankind and for nature, and loves both. Therefore, God requires that humankind respects the rights of all the creation, that humankind does not invade the spheres of other creatures, and that they behave and act in harmony with the whole universe.

Conclusion

Thus, in conclusion, we can say that, the Islamic faith lays great stress on improving the condition of the Earth at the hands of humans, as humans are described as the vice-regents of God on Earth. What is hoped from this improvement is to guarantee bliss in the eternal life after death. This is when we utilize the laws of matter for the benefit of humanity and its happiness with justice and fairness.

Therefore, human beings are the most favored among all of God's creation and everything that has been created by God is for the utilization of human beings. God has made all the other created things subservient to human beings. But, it is the duty of every human being to deal with the creation as a loving and caring friend, so that humanity can benefit from it. Muslims all over the world have awakened to the ecological crisis that is facing the world and some of the present Day Islamic Environmental Action includes environmental activism based on Islamic principles by the Meteorology and Environmental Protection Agency in Saudi Arabia. Furthermore, the theme of the first Arab Ministerial Conference was: "The Environmental Aspects of Development" which incorporated Islamic faith.[106]

[106] "Doctrinal and Modern Ethical Resource for Ecological Concern in the Islamic Religion," http://www.hollys7.tripod.com/religionandecology.htm (01 September 2013).

Chapter 5

Appreciating Diversity of Life The Significance of the Jaina Concept of Anekāntavāda (अनेकान्तवाद) in the Milieu of Religious Fundamentalism

Gene Roddenberry, American television screenwriter, producer and creator of the original Star Trek television series, once said: "*If man is to survive, he will have learned to take a delight in the essential differences between men and between cultures. He will learn that differences in ideas and attitudes are a delight, part of life's exciting variety, not something to fear.*" We live in a world of diversity. Society is a concoction of different faiths, cultures, dialects, worldviews, creeds, doctrines, philosophies etc. While diversity can be an enriching experience, often it is seen as a threat because of our inability to recognize the right of others to have their own opinions, views, faith and traditions. This gives birth to a fear psychosis towards others resulting in fundamentalism. In a world of diversity, it is impossible to agree with everything and everyone. We must hold on to our beliefs and opinions if we are satisfied that they are based upon our own rational observations, but tolerate those of others to have their own.

Religious fundamentalism is on the rise all around the world. Indian democracy and secularism is under pressure with Hindu fundamentalists being antithetical to the very existence of religious diversity by propagating Hindu nationalism based on Hindutva ideology which emphasizes one religion, one culture, one language and one nation. Hence, in such a context there is a pertinent need to recoup religious diversities in order to maintain the secular fabric of India, for without protection of diversity, secularism cannot exist.

How can we reclaim religions in the milieu of religious fundamentalism? How can we appreciate diversity of life in order to instill peace and harmony among people of different religions? This article theorizes that religious fundamentalism can be best countered by strengthening and upholding the liberative elements of every religion that can serve as antidotes to religious fundamentalism. As asserted by John S. Augustine, we need to recognize diversity as God's gift which should be appreciated and viewed as an enriching experience and not as a threat. We require a dialogical understanding of Truth/God rather than exclusivist claims and we need to inculcate a relationship of tolerance and equal respect among people of different faiths.[107]

Jainism has a beautiful concept called *Anekāntavāda,*[108] which can be significantly helpful in cultivating an attitude of tolerance and religious harmony. Therefore, to enable people of different faiths appreciate diversity that we encounter in life so as to be able to counter constricted fundamentalist tendencies, this

---

[107] John S. Augustine, ed., *Religious Fundamentalism: An Asian Perspective* (Bangalore: SATHRI/CCA/WARC, 1993), 186.

[108] *Anekāntavāda* is a combination of two Sanskrit words *Anekānta* and *vāda* which means "non-one-sidedness" or "many-sidedness." It has also been interpreted to mean non-absolutism, "intellectual Ahimsa", as well as a rejection of fanaticism that leads to terror attacks and mass violence. It will be dealt in detail in section 3 of this paper.

paper is an attempt to draw out the significance of the Jaina concept of *Anekāntavāda* in the milieu of religious fundamentalism.

1. Jainism: A Brief Overview

Etymologically, the word 'Jain' is derived from the Sanskrit *ji* (to conquer) and hence *jina* (conqueror).[109] According to Jain tradition, the timeless truths enshrined in their religion were given expression by a long line of 24 *Jinas*, also called *tīrthañkaras.*[110] The *Jinas* (Conquerors, victors) are so called because they are the ones who conquered the *samsara* (the cycle of births and deaths) and the passions which bind the souls to *samsara.*[111]

Although, Mahāvira is commonly considered to be the founder of Jainism, it would be improper to firmly call Mahāvira as the 'founder of Jainism' because the first *tīrthañkara* of the present time cycle is Rṣabha who lived millions of years ago. Moreover, although not much is known about the first 22 *tīrthañkaras*, the last two Pārsva (ca. 817 BCE) and Mahāvira (ca. 540-468 BCE) the 24th *tīrthañkara* are believed to be historical personalities and Mahāvira was the last advocate of this teaching. So, the Jains do not consider Mahāvira as the founder of their religion. He was only a reformer and revivalist of the faith taught by the earlier *tīrthañkaras.*[112] Jainism, although not popularly known beyond the frontiers of India, has much to offer in terms of its philosophy and ethical teachings.

An independent and primeval religion of India, Jainism was believed to grow as an exodus from and revolt against Vedic Brahmanism. However, recent researches have proved that certain

---

[109] Susanaga Weeraperuma, *Major Religions of India* (Delhi: Motilal Banarsidass Publishers, 1985), 27. Hereafter cited as Weeraperuma, *Major Religions...*

[110] *Tīrthañkara* means "ford-maker" because they are regarded as the ford-makers across the ocean of *samsara.*

[111] P. S. Daniel, "The Jaina Religious Tradition," in *Religious Traditions of India*, edited by P. S. Daniel, David C. Scott and G. R. Singh (Delhi: ISPCK, 1988), 172. Hereafter cited as Daniel, *Jaina Religious Tradition...*

[112] See Weeraperuma, *Major Religions...*, 28; Daniel, *Jaina Religious Tradition...*, 172.

fundamentals of Jainism are older even than the *Rig Veda*. Jainism as well as Buddhism characterizes the principal streams of *Sramanic*[113] tradition. Jainism teaches a path to spiritual purity and enlightenment through disciplined non-violence (*ahimsa,*[114] "non-injury") to all living creatures, which is closely interlinked with the doctrine of *anekāntavāda*, which will be described in detail later on. Jainism prescribes the three jewels (*tri-ratnas*) viz. right faith (*samyak-darsana*), right knowledge (*samyak-jnāna*) and right conduct (*samyak-cāritra*) by which one can attain liberation or *moksa*. One should possess all these three in the pursuit of *moksa*.

Therefore, in a nutshell, we can say that Jainism is a religion of the courageous and the brave. It is a faith, where everyone has to work out their own salvation. Hence, those who have

---

[113] *Sramana* means "seeker, one who performs acts of austerity, ascetic." The term refers to several Indian religious movements parallel to but separate from the historical Vedic religion. Several *Sramana* movements are known to have existed in India before the 6th century BCE. It existed in parallel to, but separate from Vedic Hinduism. The *Sramanic* tradition advocated a life of absolute renunciation (*pravarjya*) and rigorous asceticism as the means of attaining liberation from the bondage of *samsara*. It was non-vedic and non-Aryan in origin and flourished in India even before the advent of the Aryans. The *Sramanic* tradition challenged the authority of the Vedas and the efficacy of animal sacrifice. They held the view that soul or life is present in all beings and respect for life is of supreme importance. See Daniel, *Jaina Religious Tradition...*, 172.

[114] *Ahimsā* (Sanskrit: अहिंसा) is a fundamental principle forming the cornerstone of Jaina ethics and doctrine. The term means nonviolence, non-injury and absence of desire to harm any life forms. All non-violent practices and rituals of Jains flow from the principle of *ahimsā*. The Jain concept of *ahimsā* is very different from the concept of nonviolence found in other philosophies. According to the Jain philosophy, violence refers primarily to injuring one's own self – behaviour which inhibits the soul's own ability to attain *moksha* (liberation from the cycle of births and deaths). At the same time it also means violence to others because it is this tendency to harm others that ultimately harms one's own soul. Furthermore, the Jains extend the concept of *ahimsā* not only to humans but to all animals, plants, micro-organisms and all beings having life or life potential. All life is sacred and everything has a right to live fearlessly to its maximum potential. Living beings need not fear those who have taken the vow of *ahimsā*.

attained enlightenment and broken the shackles of *samsara* are appropriately called as '*Jinas*' (conquerors).

2. The Jaina Concept of *Anekāntavāda*

The fundamental doctrines of Jainism can be exemplified in two words, namely *Ahimsā* and *Anekānta*, the two principles of peaceful co-existence, philosophically and socially. Dr. P. S. Lamba categorically asserts that,

> "It is no exaggeration to say that *Ahimsa* and *Anekānta* are the greatest contributions of Jainism to world thought in general and Indian thought in particular…Thus if *Ahimsa* is the flower of Jainism, *Anekānta* will be its crown… Whatever different shades of meaning these two terms may have, but to me Ahimsa is the principle of respect for life and *Anekānta* is the doctrine of open-mindedness."[115]

Sethia also argues that it was *anekāntavāda* that played a pivotal role in the survival of Jainism against the onslaught of sectarian groups and other faiths at various points of time. It allowed Jains to survive during the most hostile and unfavourable moments in history by allowing the Jain thinkers to maintain the validity of doctrine, while at the same time respectfully criticizing the views of the opponents.[116]

The word *anekāntavāda* is a compound of two Sanskrit words: *anekānta* and *vāda*. The word *anekānta* itself is composed of three root words, "*an*" (not), "*eka*" (one) and "*anta*" (end, side), together it connotes "not one ended, sided," "many-sidedness," or "manifoldness." The word *vāda* means "doctrine, way, speak, thesis." The term *anekāntavāda* is translated by scholars as the doctrine of "many-sidedness," "non-onesidedness," or "many pointedness."[117] In simple terms, *anekāntavāda* may be defined

---

[115] R. C. Dwivedi, ed., *Contribution of Jainism to Indian Culture* (Delhi: Motilal Banarsidass, 1975), 2. Hereafter cited as Dwivedi, *Contribution…*

[116] Tara Sethia, *Ahimsā, Anekānta, and Jainism* (Delhi: Motilal Banarsidass Publishers, 2004), 7-8. Hereafter cited as Sethia, *Ahimsa…*

[117] https://en.wikipedia.org/wiki/Anekantavada (September 23, 2019)

as the method of viewing or explaining a thing from different standpoints. It is the method of honestly accepting and reconciling the apparently contradictory attributes in a thing from different standpoints.[118]

Therefore, the term *anekāntavāda* means the theory of non-onesidedness or, more precisely, 'the theory of many-sided nature of reality.' The basic connotation is that reality is essentially *anekāntic* (many-sided) in character. Thus, the doctrine of *anekāntavāda* can be described as acceptance of the manifoldness of reality. No philosophic proposition, as it claims, can be true if it is simply put without any qualification. If a proposition is asserted unconditionally, it excludes other rival possibilities and then it becomes *ekānta* (one sided). Such unconditional assertion violates the principle of *anekānta* and thus, it is to be regarded as false.[119]

The doctrine of *Anekānta* holds that reality is many-sided and that it is possible to look at reality from diverse stand-points. All the theories of reality that acknowledges only one aspect of reality while rejecting all others is *ekānta* (one-sided). *Anekānta* on the other hand, takes into account all the diverse facets of reality into consideration and presents a synthetic view of reality, which comprehends all the absolutistic or one-sided theories.[120] Reality, for the Jains, is complex not simply in the sense of constituting manyness (*aneka*) but also because of its manifoldness (*Anekānta*). It does not simply maintain that there are many reals, but also accepts that each of the reals is so complex that it is difficult to

---

[118] Nagin J. Shah, trans., *Jaina Philosophy and Religion: English translation of Jaina Darsana by Munisri Nyayavijayaji* (Delhi: Bhogilal Lehar Chand Institute of Indology, 1998), 328. Hereafter cited as Shah, *Jaina Philosophy...*

[119] Alok Tandon, "Anekantavada and Ahimsa: A Framework for Interreligious Dialogue," *Indian Philosophical Quarterly XXIX No I* (January 2002): 106. Hereafter cited as Tandon, *Anekantavada and Ahimsa...*

[120] K. P. Sinha, *The Philosophy of Jainism* (Calcutta: Punthi Pustak, 1990), 9.

understand it fully.[121] Every object possesses innumerable positive and negative characters. Hence, it is impossible for ordinary people to know all the qualities of a thing. We can know only some qualities of some things. In order to know all the characteristics of a thing, one needs to become omniscient (*kevalin*). Therefore, he/she who knows all the qualities of one thing knows all the qualities of all things, and he/she who knows all the qualities of all things, knows all the qualities of one thing.[122] He/She is a *Kevalin* (Omniscient being) and possesses *kevala jnana* (Omniscience).

According to Jainism, since reality is so complex in structure it perplexes all endeavors to describe it directly and once for all. Hence, the limitation of a particular judgment and the feasibility of different judgments from other points of view must always be kept in mind.[123] Jainism teaches that every judgment that we pass in our daily life about any object is true only in reference to the standpoint occupied and the aspect of the object considered. Since we tend to forget this limitation and regard our judgments as unconditionally true, we come to quarrel and disagree very often in life.[124]

According to the doctrine of *anekāntavāda*, matter and spirit are two distinct realities, eternal, infinite, different and detached from each other. An object is made out of the combination of these two eternal realities. Thus, each object has innumerable characteristics or qualities which cannot be wholly comprehended by the relative and limited human intellect, except by those who have attained *kevala jnana*.

---

[121] S. Gopalan, *Outlines of Jainism* (New Delhi: Wiley Eastern Limited, 1975), 145.

[122] Chandradhar Sharma, *A Critical Survey of Indian Philosophy* (Delhi: Motilal Banarsidass Publishers, 1987), 50-51. Hereafter cited as Sharma, *Critical Survey...*

[123] N. N. Bhattacharya, *Jainism A Concise Encyclopaedia* (New Delhi: Manohar Publishers & Distributors, 2009), 30. Hereafter cited as Bhattacharya, *Encyclopaedia...*

[124] Satischandra Chatterjee and Dhirendramohan Datta, *An Introduction to Indian Philosophy* (New Delhi: Rupa Publications India Private Limited, 2007), 75.

Of the infinite characteristics of a substance, there are some which are permanent and essential, and some which are accidental and subject to changes. The permanent and essential ones are called '*gunas*' and the changing and accidental ones are called '*paryayas.*' It is the combination of these two that makes all basic substances. As a result, any reality, at any time is both singular and plural to a certain extent.[125] Substance and *gunas* (attributes) are inseparable because attributes are the permanent essence of the substance and thereby inseparable. But, *paryayas* (modes) are changing and accidental. Therefore, when viewed from the viewpoint of substance, a thing is one and permanent and real. However, when viewed from the viewpoint of modes, it is many, momentary and unreal.[126]

For example, on seeing a black earthen jar in a room at a particular time, it should not be unconditionally asserted that 'the jar exists.' Rather, it should be said that 'perhaps the jar exists,' which should remind us that the existence of the jar is true only with regard to the condition of space, time, quality, etc., under which the jar exists. This prevents the inerrant judgment that the pot exists at all times or in all places. Moreover, an object may be described by a judgment which predicates of it any of the characters it possesses; or it may be described negatively, which denies of its characters belonging to other objects but absent in this.[127] Jains insist on the conditional or relative character of both affirmative and negative judgments. Therefore, when we say, 'may be this is a jar,' it is only in the sense of its existence at a particular place and time and with a particular description. Further, when we say 'maybe, the jar is red', the redness or blackness may depend on the perception of the jar under certain factors of light and darkness. So, every object *is* in one sense and *is not* in another sense. While the opposition between the predicates *is* and *is not* is reconciled, when they are thought of as characterizing an object successively, the nature of the object becomes indescribable (*avaktavya*). The

[125] Yulios, *Message of Religions...,* 134.

[126] Sharma, *Critical Survey...,* 51.

[127] Bhattacharya, *Encyclopaedia...,* 30.

colour of the jar may be black when raw and red after it is baked. But, if one asks, what is the real colour of the jar always and under all conditions, the only reply would be, 'it is indescribable.'

The manifoldness of reality makes it impossible for an ordinary person to comprehend all its characteristics. This means many limitations, extensions, relations, points of view. A thing may be known from various angles and all such views may be correct in their own limitations. Therefore, *anekāntavāda* keeps a knower in his/her own limitation. So, whenever he/she crosses his/her own limitation and declares his/her knowledge as right and complete and that of the other as totally wrong and incomplete, he/she commits *himsa* (violence, injury). Thus *anekāntavāda* saves one from self-righteousness and from committing injury to oneself as well as to others. It guides how to present the limited knowledge as limited or incomplete. Persons with other viewpoints do not feel vulnerable; they do not feel that they are wrong. Thus, both sides try to understand the views of each other and thereby enter into a dialogue, which results in tolerance and respect for the views of others. This created an intellectual atmosphere which may lead to, if possible, a new synthesis, if not possible, to a peaceful co-existence.

Anekāntavāda is characterized by toleration, understanding and respect for the views of others. This does not mean that one does not have any view or standpoint, but a sincere attempt is made to understand the position of the adversary, in accordance with the ontology one holds dear. To mistake any one-sided and incomplete view as the entire truth is to fall into the error of *ekāntavāda* or one-sidedness. Since Jainism takes into account all these partial views, it is called *Anekāntavāda*.

Critics have criticized *Anekāntavāda* saying that, it is not a doctrine of certainty, but a doctrine of uncertainty, skepticism since it describes a thing as both permanent and impermanent, existent and non-existent, etc., at one and the same time. But, this criticism is wrong and baseless. For example, when one sees a rope in a dark night, there arises doubt in the mind: 'Is this a rope or a snake?' The intellect goes on dithering between two options, viz. a rope and a serpent, unable to ascertain one, excluding the other. But, such kind of doubt is not found in *Anekāntavāda*.

Anekāntavāda requires of us to examine a thing from different standpoints and to ascertain its particular attribute from a particular standpoint. Upon examining a thing from various standpoints, one understands that it is "certainly existent from one standpoint and certainly non-existent from another standpoint; similarly, it is certainly permanent from one standpoint and certainly impermanent from another standpoint. A thing is certainly existent from the standpoint of its own substance, place, time and attribute, and certainly non-existent from the standpoint of alien substance, etc. It is certainly permanent from the standpoint of its substance, and certainly impermanent from the standpoint of its modes."[128] In order to clarify this, an example may be given thus:

Syād nitya eva ghaṭaḥ, syād anitya eva ghaṭaḥ/ (From a certain point of view, the pot is certainly permanent; from a certain point of view, the pot is certainly impermanent). The particle '*eva*' denotes 'certainty' or 'without doubt.' It is not the uncertainty of judgment, but the conditional or relative character that is expressed by the particle *syād* (may be). Subject to the conditions under which a judgment is made, the judgment is valid. So, there is no room for skepticism. All that is implied is that every assertion which is true is true only under certain conditions.[129] Therefore, *Anekāntavāda* is not uncertainty; it is not skepticism, but the doctrine of conditional certainty.

3. Understanding Religious Fundamentalism

The word 'Fundamentalism' in a wide sense refers to 'the strict following of the fundamental doctrines of any religion or system of thought.'[130] But, it is currently used in very varied senses, such that a correspondent in *The Times* has written, "I am yet to meet

---

[128] Shah, *Jaina Philosophy*...344.

[129] Shah, *Jaina Philosophy*..., 344-345.

[130] Catherine Soanes, ed., et.al., *Compact Oxford Dictionary, Thesaurus, and Wordpower Guide* (Oxford: Oxford University Press, Indian Edition, 15th impression, 2005), 364.

two fundamentalists who can agree on an exact definition of fundamentalism."[131]

According to Sr. Stella Baltazar, "Fundamentalism implies a belief held by a group of people who have the power and the facility to impose, project their beliefs on others and control them with an ulterior personal motive which negates and denies access to such facilities and information to a section of people in its own circle or outside of it. When a group uses the name of God in doing this, it becomes Religious Fundamentalism."[132] Historically, the term 'Fundamentalism' originated from the sphere of Protestant Christians.[133] Thus, we can say that 'Fundamentalism' refers to the movement of the conservatives against the liberals in order to uphold and preserve the original principles of a religious faith. It also implies returning to the basic teachings of any religion. Even though the term 'Fundamentalism' was first used as a deliberate reaction to liberalism, it has come to have a pejorative connotation in the minds of the common people.

Today, 'Fundamentalism' has come to have a mostly negative implication. Therefore, according to L. Legrand, 'religious fundamentalism' is, "no purely spiritual and religious phenomenon, rather it has deep socio-anthropological roots, and thus appears as the expression of a quest for security which is no longer provided by the surrounding society and religious establishment."[134] Whereas for Vincent Shekhar, religious

---

[131] J. I. Packer, *'Fundamentalism' and the Word of God* (Grand Rapids, Michigan: William B. Eerdmans Publishing Company, 1958), 24.

[132] Stella Baltazar, 'Religious Fundamentalism: A Feminist Perspective,' in John S. Augustine, ed., *Religious Fundamentalism: An Asian Perspective* (Bangalore: SATHRI/CCA/WARC, 1993), 97.

[133] When we look at the historical origin of this term, we find that, the term Fundamentalism originated from the sphere of the Protestant Christians in U.S.A. in the year between 1909 and 1915 with a series of pamphlets called 'The Fundamentals: A testimony to the Truth' which attacked modernist or liberal views of the Bible and defending fundamental doctrines. Ninian Smart, *The World's Religions* (Cambridge: Cambridge University Press, 1989), 365.

[134] A. Peter Abir, ed., *Biblical Apostolate and Religious Fundamentalism* (Chennai: Catholic Bishop Federation, 2004), 12.

fundamentalism is "a threat posed by ideologies and movements that its feelings and structures are often manipulates by political, economic, cultural or ethnic power groups in order to safeguard their vested interests."[135]

Fundamentalism now has come to designate one's own position as the only valid position. It rears a false consciousness among members of a particular group placing emphasis on the most minor and marginal details of a tradition, often forgetting the dynamic orientation of faith to the ultimate meaning of human life.[136] However, Ram Puniyani categorically asserts that we must distinguish between orthodoxy and fundamentalism as there are millions who harmlessly follow orthodox traditions of different religions without harming anyone in the society. Similarly, we also need to differentiate between communalism and fundamentalism.[137] Therefore, in popular usage, the term 'fundamentalism' has come to mean the narrow-minded claim that one's faith is the sole truth while opposing others' belief, faith or opinion and 'religious fundamentalists' as the people who are terrorizing and causing immense trouble to their fellow human beings in the name of religion.

---

[135] Vincent Sekhar, *Quest for Harmony: An Anthology of Religions in Dialogue* (Bangalore: Claretian Publications, 2002), 212.

[136] V. S. Lalrinawma, *Missiological Issues Facing the Contemporary Church in India* (Bangalore: Centre for Contemporary Christianity, 2011), 196. Hereafter cited as V. S. Lalrinawma, *Missiological Issues...*

[137] According to Puniyani, while communalism is mainly concerned with political or economic interests of a particular community, fundamentalism is enforcement of sectarianism with all rigidity for political mobilization of a community to satisfy the power-goals of its elite. While communalism is the exploitation of sentiments of a religion-based community for a secular goal (political power), fundamentalism is enforcing narrow sectarian practices for strengthening religious orthodoxy as well as achieving political power. Ram Puniyani, "Religion, Politics and Fundamentalism," in Sentiwate Aier and Limatula Longkumer, eds., *Reclaiming Diversities in Secular India: Theological Response to Religious Fundamentalism* (Kolkata: SATHRI, 2019), 37-38.

Although Religious Fundamentalism has many characteristics, Paul Puthanangady has listed out four main characteristics of religious fundamentalism as follows:[138]

(a) It rejects change in the expressions of religious faith in social structure.
(2) It tends to isolate itself from the influence of other religions, ideologies, etc.
(3) It develops an attitude of self-righteousness in people who claim to be the defenders of their faith.
(4) It considers proselytism as an integral part of its religiosity.

Thus, we can say that religious fundamentalism is a prejudiced affirmation of the truth of one's own beliefs. It is the firm conviction that one's belief is the sole truth and the desire to impose this belief on others through violent means or any other method applicable, giving scant importance or respect to the opinion of others.

However, it must be understood that religion per se is not responsible for religious fundamentalism. Rather it is the exploitation of religion for communal considerations of power and privilege that has resulted in the present appalling religio-political scenario of India. Moreover, it cannot be denied that there are expressions of religious fundamentalism in all religious traditions.[139] Due to the bane of religious fundamentalism, religion has ceased to be a meaningful faith; it has been turned into an unreasonable fixation. It is no longer a vision of life; it is being made to serve as a devious ploy. It is not a project for establishing a just society but a vehicle for the enhancement of the ruling

---

[138] Paul Puthanangady, *Challenges of Fundamentalism in Biblical Apostolate* in *Biblical Apostolate and Religious Fundamentalism* (Chennai: Catholic Bishop Federation, 2004), 119.

[139] Roger Gaikwad, "Why Study Religions? Reclaiming Religions in the Context of Religious Fundamentalism," in Lalchawiliana Varte and K. Lalchhuanawma, eds., *Religion and Women: Pilgrims in Search of Justice and Equity* (Aizawl: Lengchhawn Press, 2018), 10.

class.[140] Fundamentalism has reduced religion to tyranny, where the fanatical groups have subjected the religious minority of India to religious persecution. Religious extremism breeds sectarian violence and fanaticism.[141]

The consequences of religious fundamentalism on a pluralistic society especially India is quite obvious and noticeable; although some may be quite subtle and hidden. But, nevertheless, it touches the life of the nation at different points. Religious Fundamentalism has become a dangerous weapon in the hands of politicians and politicized fundamentalism has several detrimental consequences.

The consequences of religious fundamentalism may be enumerated as follows:[142]

- Religious fundamentalism, with its political implications, is a serious threat to the secular and democratic character of the Indian state.
- It disturbs the plurality of India's cultural life which for many centuries has nourished the life of people of various ethnic groups, religions and languages.
- Fundamentalism goes against the rights and privileges of minority religious communities. It ignores the fact that religious minorities have been in India for many centuries and have made significant contributions to the life of the country, particularly to its cultural life.

---

[140] Asghar Ali Engineer, "Islamic Fundamentalism and Communalism in India," in *Religion and Asian Politics: An Islamic Perspective* (Hong Kong: Christian Conference of Asia-International Affairs, 1985), 91.

[141] V. S. Lalrinawma, *Missiological Issues...*, 197, 199.

[142] See Stanley J. Samartha, "The Causes and Consequences of Religious Fundamentalism," in *Fundamentalism and Secularism: The Indian Predicament*, edited by Andreas Nehring (Madras: Gurukul Lutheran Theological College and Research Institute, 1994), 38; Gnana Robinson, "Why is Fundamentalism a Problem Today?," in *Fundamentalism and Secularism: The Indian Predicament,* edited by Andreas Nehring (Madras: Gurukul Lutheran Theological College and Research Institute, 1994),

- It promotes self-righteous arrogance which discriminates against other people, and thus poses a threat to the harmonious living of people of different origins, races, colour and faiths.
- It endorses lack of justice concerns, since equality is not part of their faith, justice for all is also not part of their concern.

4. The Significance of *Anekāntavāda* in the Milieu of Religious Fundamentalism

Humanity is on the verge of collapsing due to lack of understanding, which includes understanding ourselves and each other. Today, if one person does not agree with me, he/she is wicked. There seems to be no half-way, no neutrality.[143] Many authors like Kamala Jain, have proposed that the Jaina tradition with its emphasis on *Ahimsā* and *Anekānta* is able to provide a solution to a host of problems like religious intolerance, terrorism, wars, depletion of natural resources, environmental degradation, and so on which the world is facing.[144] Religious fundamentalism simply put, is an intolerant affirmation of the truth of one's own beliefs, the firm conviction that one's principle is the sole truth. It is the conviction that those who share my beliefs are good and those who do not are wicked and evil. Hence, it implies the desire to impose this belief on others through violent means or any other method applicable, giving scant importance or respect to the outlook of others.

However, the doctrine of *Anekāntavāda* with its concept of the many-sidedness of reality seems to have certain significances to counter religious fundamentalism. Therefore, attempt will be made to draw out significances of the doctrine of *Anekāntavāda* in the milieu of religious fundamentalism.

a) Learning to Accommodate Diversity, Adaptability, Flexibility and Open-mindedness: We live in a world of

---

[143] Nagin J. Shah, ed., *Jaina Theory of Multiple Facets of Reality and Truth (Anekāntavāda)* (Delhi: Bhogilal Leharchand Institute of Indology, 2000), 128. Hereafter cited as Shah, *Theory*...

[144] Sethia, *Ahimsa*..., 113.

plurality. Life is largely a matter of compromises and adjustments. To experience peace and happiness, you must be adaptable and flexible to the demands of life, without sacrificing your values and ideals. It can happen only when you have tolerance, respect, and openness. As human beings, we need to coexist with others, overcome divisive thinking, avoiding frivolous conflicts, judgmental attitude, and make peace with ourselves and the world around us.

The concept of *Anekāntavāda* may be utilized to learn to accommodate diversity, overcome attraction and aversion to things, and become equal to the world around you. It is not difficult with compassion and understanding to cultivate an accommodative and expansive mind that can assimilate contradictions and bear with the burdens of life, the mistakes of others, and the shortcomings of your own behavior.

Anekāntavāda may also be referred to as the doctrine of open-mindedness. It is based on the conviction that a thing is constituted of varied aspects and to understand it properly, one needs to consider as many viewpoints as possible. The comprehension of a thing from different points of view develops a catholic outlook which is crucial for peaceful co-existence. This doctrine has helped Jainism to appreciate the view-points of others in the field of philosophy. What *Anekāntavāda* condemns is the one-sided obstinate and inflexible approach to a thing, which is the root cause of incongruity. Open-mindedness inculcates generosity of spirit and balance of mind. Hence, *Anekāntavāda* creates open-mindedness which is the necessary basis for lessening tensions between nations, people of different religions and cultural backgrounds and develops an attitude of intellectual honesty.

b) It Discards Absolutism, Upholds Multi-dimensionality of Truth and Neutrality in the Field of Thought: Since things have multi characters, they are the objects of all-sided knowledge. The comprehension that takes into account the full meaning of an object through only one-sided knowledge is partial knowledge. *Anekāntavāda* exhorts us to reject all absolute judgments, or else truth would be violated. Reality has got innumerable characteristics. A valid knowledge is defined as that which gives us knowledge of a thing in all its aspects. All expressions are in one way or the other real. All objects have innumerable characters, therefore all things are multi-dimensional or *anekāntic.*

'*Anekāntavāda*' reminds us that '*ekāntavāda*' may not be able to fully contain the infinite characteristics of an object. It rejects the fundamentalistic thinking "*Only I am right; everyone else or everything else is wrong.*" Religious fundamentalism cancels out the existence of other view-points. It is grounded on the firm conviction that one's view point is the absolute truth. However, *anekāntavāda* makes us realize that there are other points of view which must be accepted or acknowledged, or at the least appreciated. This is possible only when one puts oneself into another's position. This is called sympathy which is the act of reproducing in our minds the feelings of others.

It is well known that there is a thin line between distinguishing what is right and what is wrong. *Anekāntavāda* says that no *ism* can claim absolute truth for itself, and no *ism* can be condemned as absolutely wrong. Every statement has an intermixture of right and wrong. We have to adopt, an attitude of neutrality towards two apparently contradictory statements. It is not a case of indecisiveness but a case of clear understanding of what is right and what is wrong in a statement. When we look at things from this angle, there would be no reason for dispute.[145]

c) Towards Tolerant or Flexible Fundamentalism: The Jaina tradition may be considered 'fundamentalist' in the sense that its cosmology and ethics have not been subject to revision. However, tolerant or flexible fundamentalism, preferred by the Jainas, allows and in fact requires that the religiously informed person be well acquainted with how different traditions have approached the basic issues of human limitation and transcendence. It encourages respect for others' perspectives and yet allows one's primary commitment to remain rooted in that which one feels most genuine. This approach allows for various possibilities, but does not deny or relativize the validity of one's own position. It also

[145] Dwivedi, *Contribution...*, 125.

allows traditions and persons to discover commonalities without indicating those commonalities as absolutes.[146]

Fundamentalism is often viewed critically as a blind devotion to a fixed set of beliefs to the point of excluding all other views. However, in order for a religious tradition to perform effectively, the adherents need to adhere to certain world views which may be conflicting with others at times. A solution to this predicament is found in the Jaina rational frame-work that allows for and respects innumerable positions yet holds to its own cosmological and ethical view. Thus, the Jaina model of flexible fundamentalism through the doctrine of *anekāntavāda* offers alternative for authenticating a fundamentalist devotion to basic teachings while still acknowledging the legitimacy of differing views within their own context.

d) Towards a Horizontal Model of Inclusivism: Halbfass calls *anekāntavāda* a "horizontal model" of inclusivism. It is through a horizontal plane of view that we will be able to keep all relevant elements of other traditions in view without a hierarchical or superiority attitude while at the same time, holding on to our own faith traditions. Jainism is willing to put the Jain tradition on par with other religious traditions at the same time not incorporating other beliefs into their own fixed system. As far as the intentions are concerned, it is one of open-mindedness, the willingness to open the boundaries of their own system to include the truths of other traditions. *Anekāntavāda* enables us to have a very harmonious attitude towards followers of other religions that could be considered to be a spirit of tolerance.[147]

This horizontal model of inclusivism through the doctrine of *Anekāntavāda* can protect diverse faith traditions from being intolerantly fundamental and at the same time from slipping into a self-destructive relativism, because on a metaphysical level, the doctrine of *Anekāntavāda* maintains that only the non-one-sided faith can be the superior faith.

---

[146] Tandon, *Anekantavada and Ahimsa...,* 113.

[147] Melanie Barbato, *Jain Approaches to Plurality: Identity as Dialogue* (Netherlands: Brill, 2018), 124.

e) Towards a Framework of Intellectual *Ahimsa*: In a pluralistic context, fundamentalist tendencies may be offensive for others who might feel threatened. At the same time, if one does not hold on to a particular view, that means he/she is baseless, without purpose or identity. Both fundamentalism and baselessness are *ekāntic* and violate the principles of *Ahimsa.* Therefore, instead of absolutism or utter relativism, what is necessary is to develop a framework that combines tolerance with definiteness in commitment to one's own traditions. Thus, in the context of religious fundamentalism, what is imperative is to develop a framework where persons with conflicting cosmologies and ideologies tolerate each other, respect each other, and coexist harmoniously.

As has been mentioned earlier, the Jaina tradition can be considered to be strictly 'fundamentalist.' However, through the doctrine of *Anekāntavāda,* Jains have exercised great care in articulating how their position differs from that of others, at the same time, not condemning alternate views as incorrect…but only incomplete. Jains have exhibited great care to understand and to respect the position of others. As a result, they have been engaged in dialogue with others which has enhanced their knowledge without altering their own faith and commitment. Alok Tandon has proposed a framework for inter-religious dialogue from which we can delineate the salient features for the framework of intellectual *Ahimsa.*[148] The study of *Anekāntavāda* in the previous sections shows that reality is manifold in character (*Anekāntic*). Therefore, for limited human beings grasping the comprehensive view of reality is impossible. Thus, no one statement can ever account for totality of reality. As a result, it is incorrect to hold on to any extreme view. When we comprehend the diversity and vastness of reality, then we negate religious bigotry and fundamentalism and inculcate intellectual *Ahimsa* which fosters tolerance, respect, appreciation, peaceful and harmonious co-existence of different faiths. Inculcating intellectual *Ahimsa* would inevitably manifest

[148] Tandon, *Anekantavada and Ahimsa...,* 111.

in physical *Ahimsa* leading to peace and harmony towards all human beings as well as the entire creation.

5. Appreciating Diversity: Challenges for Christianity

Any follower of Hinduism, Buddhism, Jainism will be comfortable with the idea that there is some truth in other religions, including Christianity because accommodation is fundamental to the Indian religious psyche. It is this spirit of tolerance that has enabled India to survive with so many cultures and religions. This led Swami Vivekananda, one of India's great thinkers, to say, "Let noble truths come to us from all corners." For the Indian mind, truth claims of other religions are not threatening but enriching.[149]

Christianity has come a very long way with regards to its view and attitude towards people of other faiths. However, Christianity with its claim that other religions are in need of the illumination that can come only through the knowledge of what God has done for humanity in Christ and the claim of salvation in the belief and acceptance of Jesus Christ alone as personal Lord and Saviour poses a very big challenge in a pluralistic society like India to appreciate the prevailing diversity. These exclusive claims of Christianity are seen to be patronizing, a claim of superiority, which is difficult to be tolerated by the people of other faiths. Therefore Christians are challenged to realize that, in the pluralistic landscape of India there are no gaps to fill—there is only room for enriching each other. So, we need to find some way of connecting Christian faith narratives with those of others. They should be connected in such a way that they lead to the God of the Bible who calls people to him through Jesus Christ.[150]

There are two possible ways of connecting our religious discourses depending on what type of conjunctions one would

---

[149] Paulson Pulikottil, *The Challenge of Accommodation in Religiously Plural India*, https://fullerstudio.fuller.edu/the-challenge-of-accommodation-in-religiously-plural-india/ (17 October 2019).

[150] Paulson Pulikottil, *The Challenge of Accommodation in Religiously Plural India*, https://fullerstudio.fuller.edu/the-challenge-of-accommodation-in-religiously-plural-india/ (17 October 2019).

like to use. The choice seems to be between "no, but" or "yes, and." The first choice is to see a discontinuity between world religions and Christianity. The second is to see Christianity as the fulfillment of human longing that other religions witness to.[151]

What is specifically Christian in a pluralistic context is the uniqueness of Christ and his message, the newness of life in Christ, new creation or new being in Christ. The purpose of the Christian faith is to transform humankind and society in Christ and this transformation is brought about by the Holy Spirit. Christians and Christianity need to stress that the uniqueness of Christ and his message is not exclusive, because the essence of inter-religious dialogue is to "give and take." The spiritual riches of the Indian culture must be integrated into the Christian life and the Christian message has to purify, elevate and perfect the Indian religio-moral values.[152]

When people value diversity, they recognize and respect differences. Stereotypes, prejudice, and discrimination interfere with this respect and come about when people fear difference. As Christians living in pluralistic context, we are challenged to appreciate diversity by increasing our understanding of our own and others' worldview by examining critically our attitudes towards people who are different from us. When we identify the origin of our negative reactions and recognize our biases. By willing to talk, listen, and learn; being aware how discrimination operates, who it privileges, and who it harms. By respecting and accepting differences, we can understand the liberative motifs present in other faith traditions. We will be able to see that socio-cultural and religious diversity is a gift of God that needs to be enjoyed and appreciated. Appreciating and celebrating this diversity in our daily lives can help us all lead happier, peaceful, harmonious and more productive lives.

---

[151] Paulson Pulikottil, *The Challenge of Accommodation in Religiously Plural India*, https://fullerstudio.fuller.edu/the-challenge-of-accommodation-in-religiously-plural-india/ (17 October 2019).

[152] Mariasusai Dhavamony, *Christian Theology of Inculturation,* (Rome: Gregorian Biblical BookShop, 1997), 165.

Conclusion

Behind almost all acts of religious intolerance and fundamentalism lies a superiority attitude towards other faith traditions and non-acceptance of the views and opinions held by others. In the contemporary pluralistic scenario, it is impractical as well as not feasible to expect people of all faiths to give up their belief in the superiority of their respective faith traditions. However, religious intolerance and fundamentalism to a very large extent can be curtailed if adherents of different religions can accept that there is some amount of truth in the belief system of others. The Jaina doctrine of *Anekāntavāda* exhorts us to lower our defenses and open up the margins of our faith system in order to incorporate, or at least appreciate and respect the truths of other faiths. *Anekāntavāda* will enable us to foster tolerance, respect and appreciation, peaceful and harmonious co-existence of different faiths.

Chapter 6

Each for Equal[153] Sikhism for Gender Equity

Introduction

The status of women in a society is a significant reflection of the level of social justice in that society. Women's status is often described in terms of their level of income, employment, education, health and fertility as well as their roles within the family, the community and society. In spite of the technological and intellectual development and advancements, the enactment of various laws for safeguarding the rights and privileges of women, they continue to be discriminated, oppressed and suppressed due to several historical, religious and other reasons. Throughout the history of humankind, women have suffered greatly in patriarchal and male dominated societies due to social customs and misunderstanding of religion. On one hand she was being given the credit as the better half of man and on the other, she was

[153] Each for Equal is the theme of International Women's Day 2020.

being considered a temptress, a niggling impediment in the path of the man's spiritual journey.

At the time of Guru Nanak, Indian women were severely degraded and oppressed by society. They were not provided with the privilege of education or freedom to make decisions. The presence and participation of women in religious, political social, cultural and economic affairs was virtually non-existent. Women's function was only to procreate, do household work and serve the male members of society. Female infanticide was common and the practice of *sati*, the immolation of the wife on her husband's funeral pyre, was encouraged, and sometimes even forced.[154]

In addition to teachings against caste distinction and other social evils, Guru Nanak revolutionized societal attitude towards women with his teachings. He condemned the treatment meted out to women saying that it is the women who give birth to man; it is she who makes the kings and other great men. Therefore, without woman, man is incomplete. In Medieval India, during the Sikh Guru period, the teachings of Sikh Gurus revolutionized the structure of society, institution of marriage and the role of woman in the society. Sikhism enabled woman to regain her lost glory and status not only within the four walls of the home, but in every sphere of life. Sikhism rejected all those anti-woman notions and divinized the family life by giving new meaning to the institution of marriage. Sikhism elevated the status of woman in the society as well as religious sphere.

Therefore, Sikhism's ideology and teaching concerning gender equity seems to have great relevance in today's context where women are being discriminated, oppressed, suppressed and harassed because of their sex.

1. Gender Inequality

Gender inequality has been a social issue especially in India for centuries. It is no secret that the birth of a girl child is not

---

[154] Surinder Kaur, "Equality of Women in Sikh Ideology," *Journal of Social Sciences Research, 6/2* (December 27, 2014): 1001. Hereafter cited as Kaur, *Equality of Women...*

welcomed in India. It is also well known that the discrimination begins even before the girl child is born and sometimes she is killed before she sees the light of day. Even if she manages to see the light of day, she is killed as an infant, and this results in the highly skewed child sex ratio where for every 1000 boys in India, there are only 914 girls according to the 2011 census.[155]

Today, in the 21st century women have assumed leadership roles in every field possible. But in spite of such progress, even today, the girl child remains discriminated in most Indian households. The practice of female foeticide through sex selective abortion continues to be practiced in spite of the Prenatal Diagnostic Technique Act of 1994.[156] This discrimination continues in every sphere, such as education, health, protection or participation.

Gender equality is not only a fundamental human right, but a necessary foundation for a peaceful, prosperous and sustainable world. Providing women and girls with equal access to education, health care, decent work, and representation in political and economic decision-making processes will fuel sustainable economies and benefit societies and humanity at large. Implementing new legal frameworks regarding female equality in the workplace and the eradication of harmful practices targeted at women is crucial to ending the gender-based discrimination prevalent in many countries around the world.[157]

But, although there are more women than ever in the labour market, there are still large inequalities in some regions, with women systematically denied the same work rights as men. Sexual violence and exploitation, the unequal division of unpaid care and domestic work, and discrimination in public office all remain huge barriers. Climate change and disasters continue to have a disproportionate effect on women and children, as do conflict and migration.

---

[155] https://www.cry.org/issues-views/gender-inequality (29 March 2020).

[156] https://www.cry.org/issues-views/gender-inequality (29 March 2020).

[157] https://www.un.org/sustainabledevelopment/gender-equality/ (29 March 2020).

According to the facts and figures given by the United Nations Development Programme (UNDP):[158]

- Women earn only 77 cents for every dollar men get for the same work.
- 35% of women have experienced physical and/or sexual violence.
- Women represent just 13% of agricultural landholders.
- Almost 750 million women and girls alive today were married before their 18th birthday.
- Two thirds of developing countries have achieved gender parity in primary education.
- Only 24 percent of national parliamentarians were women as of November 2018, a small increase from 11.3 percent in 1995.

In spite of several developments, achieving gender equity in every walk of life still remains a herculean task in today's world. The need of the hour is to make a change in the mindset of the society and destroy the prejudices that damage the future of the girl child. What is required is a concerted effort to sensitize the society in eradicating this issue of gender inequality.

2. A Brief Overview of Sikhism

Sikhism is the fifth largest organized religion in the world and is founded on the teachings of Guru Nanak and nine successive Gurus. Sikhism as a distinctive religious tradition began and developed over the last five centuries and especially during the life time of Guru Nanak (1469-1539) and extended up to early 18th century.

The word 'Sikhism' has been derived from the word 'Sikh,' which in turn has been derived from the Sanskrit word '*sishya*' which means 'disciple' or 'learner,' or '*siksha*' which means

[158] https://www.undp.org/content/undp/en/home/sustainable-development-goals/goal-5-gender-equality.html (29 March 2020).

'teaching.'[159] Therefore, the Sikhs may be defined as "the disciples who believe in the teaching of the ten Sikh Gurus and who venerate The Guru Granth Sahib as their sacred scripture."[160] A unique key feature of Sikhism is its belief in a non-anthropomorphic concept of God. Sikhism recommends the pursuit of salvation through trained, personal meditation on the name and content of God. Sikhs are expected to follow the instructions of the ten Sikh Gurus and their Holy Scripture, the Guru Granth Sahib. It was the tenth Guru, Gobind Singh, who decreed that the Guru Granth Sahib was the final Guru.[161]

As a result, after the death of the tenth Guru, there were no more human Gurus and the Granth Sahib is considered to be the sole Guru. While compiling the scripture, the fifth Sikh Guru, Guru Arjan Dev incorporated not only the writings of the Sikh Gurus, but also included selected works of many devotees and saints from diverse socio-economic and religious backgrounds, who believed in the unity of God and denounced caste and superstition.

Today, majority of the Sikh population live in India concentrated in the province of Punjab. During the zenith of the British *Raj*, enterprising Sikhs sought new jobs overseas and migrated to England, Kenya, Fiji, Malaysia, Thailand, Singapore, New Zealand, Australia, Canada and the United States and Sikhism spread all over the world. Britain has now the largest Sikh Community outside India.[162] Sikhs number over 14 million, with another 3 or 4 million living outside India. Of the 14 million living in India, over 60 per cent are concentrated in their home state of Punjab. There are other significant Sikh concentration in Haryana, Himachal Pradesh, Uttaranchal and Delhi. Sizeable

---

[159] Sardar Harjeet Singh, *Faith and Philosophy of Sikhism* (Delhi: Kalpaz Publications, 2009), 1. Hereafter cited as Harjeet, *Faith and Philosophy...*

[160] Godwin R. Singh, "The Sikh Religious Tradition," in *Religious Tradition of India*, edited by P. S. Daniel, David C. Scott and G. R. Singh (New Delhi: ISPCK, 1988), 312. Herafter cited as Godwin, *The Sikh...*

[161] Harjeet, *Faith and Philosophy...*

[162] Godwin, *The Sikh...*, 312.

Sikh populations can be found in North-America, Europe and Australia.[163]

3. Each for Equal: Sikhism for Gender Equity

In Hindu society woman was a prime cause of ritual pollution and in mythology she was often depicted as a fickle temptress. Guru Nanak, however, recognized that if all life originates from God, there could be no divinely created divisions of race, class, or sex. He therefore denounced Hindu and Muslim attitudes to women if they seemed to threaten their status as full human beings. This position was continued by later Gurus who condemned female infanticide, the practice of *Sati* or the giving of dowries.[164]

Many of the ancient Hindu thinkers and philosophers had very negative attitudes towards women. For Shankara[165] woman was "the gateway to hell" and for Ramanuja[166] woman is sin-born. But, Guru Nanak brought about a complete reversal of the socio-religious life and values of his time by his teaching on the equality of men and women. One of the most famous verses in the Guru Granth Sahib is that of Guru Nanak which says:

> 'It is from woman the despised one that we are conceived, it is from her that we are born. It is to woman that we are engaged and married. It is woman who is our life-long companion, and who perpetuates the race. It is she who is sought after when a man becomes a widower. We establish our social ties

[163] https://www.refworld.org/docid/49749d103c.html (17 March 2020).

[164] W. Owen Cole and Piara Singh Sambhi, *A Popular Dictionary of Sikhism* (Curzon Press: Surrey,1997), 83. Hereafter cited as Cole and Sambhi, *Popular Dictionary…*

[165] Adi Shankaracharya was an early 8th century Indian philosopher and theologian who consolidated the doctrine of Advaita Vedanta. He is credited with unifying and establishing the main currents of thought in Hinduism.

[166] Ramanuja or Ramanujacharya (1017–1157 CE) was an Indian theologian, philosopher, and one of the most important exponents of the Sri Vaishnavism tradition within Hinduism. His philosophical foundations for devotionalism were influential to the Bhakti movement. Ramanuja denied Vedic studies to women. They were not allowed to mix with men for devotion nor allowed to become nuns.

> through her. Why then condemn her from whom great men and kings are born?' (AG 473).[167]

These lines of the Adi Granth hail woman primarily as instrumentally necessary for the continuity of humankind. Guru Nanak also unequivocally challenged the prevalent Hindu view of childbirth as polluting as the following verse from the Adi Granth clearly shows:

> If pollution attaches to birth, then pollution is everywhere. Cow-dung [fuel] and firewood breed maggots; Not one grain of corn is without life; Water itself is a living substance, imparting life to all vegetation (AG 472).[168]

There was a system of keeping women isolated from the rest of the family for some days after childbirth. She was not allowed to touch anything because in doing so she would render it impure. Guru Nanak criticized this saying that everywhere reproduction is taking place. None of the things that we eat or use are free from life, which is multiplying every moment. Impurity is rather in the evil thoughts of the mind. Guru Nanak also raised his voice against the prevailing idea that a woman was impure during the days of her menstrual cycle. Nanak vehemently criticized this saying that there is no impurity in it and that it is a natural cycle. In fact, impurity is in the mouth of a person who tells lies after lies. Impurity is due to bad qualities and not due to natural bodily function. Guru Nanak also criticized the idea of a woman being impure after childbirth.[169]

Hinduism gave great importance to a celibate life and considered women equal to the *Sudras* and they were generally regarded as unfit to tread upon the spiritual path. However, Guru Nanak's logic against celibacy and his teachings on the nature and status of women was a paradigm shift from the existing notion towards women.

---

[167] Cole and Sambhi, *Popular Dictionary...,* 83.

[168] Eleanor Nesbitt, *Sikhism A Very Short Introduction* (New York: Oxford University Press Inc., 2005), 107

[169] Kaur, *Equality of Women...,* 1002.

Guru Nanak fixed five specific duties and responsibilities of the religious life and the first is to accept the equality of man and woman. Nanak was of the opinion that there is no reason to relegate women because without women there would be no one. It is the women who gave birth to great persons. This teaching of Guru Nanak was continued by the succeeding Gurus also and when the third Guru created *Manjis* or districts of religious administration, women were appointed to be in charge of some of them.[170]

There is no priesthood in Sikhism as they believe in the equality of all humankind irrespective of caste, creed or gender. However, there are certain persons who are responsible for leading the religious activities. Although, training is desirable for certain positions, anyone who is qualified, whether male or female, regardless of age or ethnic background may fill any position available.

Each of the following ten terms commonly used in Sikhism describes a particular traditional role taken in a Sikh worship service, or secular service by a religious leader, an attendant, or a Gurudwara caretaker:

Gianni, Granthi, Jethedar, Kathawak, Kirtani, Masand, Paathee, Panj Pyare, Ragi, Sevadar.[171]

Hence, in Sikhism, women have the same religious obligations as men and receive the same rewards. They are permitted to read the Guru Granth Sahib in public, to be members of the *Panj Piare*[172] and generally to dispense of any role that

---

[170] Daljeet Singh, *Essentials of Sikhism* (Singh Brothers: Amritsar, 1994)..., 86. Hereafter cited as Daljeet, *Essentials*...

[171] https://www.learnreligions.com/sikhism-clergy-terms-meanings-4590180 (28 March, 2020).

[172] On 30 March by the calendar then in use, (13 April according to the Gregorian calendar), Guru Gobind Singh instituted the Khalsa. In response to his call for Sikhs to come forward who would be willing to lay down their lives, five men eventually offered themselves. These founding members of the Khalsa have passed into history as the Panj Piare. They are Bhai Daya Singh, Bhai Dharam Singh, Bhai Himmat Singh, Bhai Mohkam Singh, Bhai Sahib Singh. The expression is also used of the executive committees appointed to look after

might be interpreted as male.[173] Women are not only allowed to read from the Guru Granth Sahib in the services in the Gurudwara, they can also join the *Khalsa* (order or community of Sikhs). When they join the *Khalsa*, Sikh men are given the name Singh (lion), while women are called Kaur (princess).[174] In practice, women have total spiritual equality with men, but the roles of men and women differ. While men are more active, women are more homely. Whatever restrictions women in Sikh society face are more of social rather than religious origin.

Conclusion

Throughout human history misogynistic notions regarding the position of women has damaged the status of women in the socio-religious and political spheres. In Medieval India also, during the time of the Sikh Gurus, such notions regarding women was prevailing with various social evils such as *Sati,* female infanticide and dowry system perpetrated against women. However, through the teachings of the Sikh Gurus, the structure of society was revolutionized and the role of women in the society and in religion was elevated. It is due to Sikhism that women could regain their lost glory and status not only within the confines of the home, but in all walks of life. Woman in Sikhism is a facilitator of the spiritual journey of man.

In a world where women are being discriminated, oppressed and suppressed simply because of their sex in every sphere of life, religion because of its strong emotional appeal has the potential to bring about change in the mindset of the people. Hence, the

---

the five Takhts, of the five people who conduct the *amrit sanskar* (initiation ceremony), the five who carry nishan sahibs before the Guru Granth Sahib in processions, and of the five people of good standing which a family may ask to eat with them on certain joyful occasions such as the birth of a child. When *karah parshad* is distributed five small portions may be rolled into balls and given to five respected members of the sangat before the rest are served. Cole and Sambhi, *Popular Dictionary...,* 65.

[173] W. H. McLeod, *The A to Z of Sikhism* (Plymouth: Scarecrow Press, Inc., 2005), 70.

[174] Harjeet, *Faith and Philosophy...,* 35.

teaching of Sikhism on the equality of men and women and the contributions that Sikhism has had in elevating the status of women challenges followers of various religious traditions to change our mindsets towards gender equity and to bring about equality between men and women in all walks of life.

Chapter 7

Religion and the Global Water Crisis
The Significance and Relevance of Water in Zoroastrianism for Today

All religions of the world confess God's presence in the cosmos, and no religion preaches use of violence against nature. All religions attribute, in varying degrees, sacredness to water, fire, mountains, rivers, trees etc., and use them symbolically in their religious worship and are mentioned in their sacred scriptures as objects dear to God and sacred to the faithful.[175] Therefore, we can say that religion has an important role to play in addressing the ecological crisis that is being faced by the world today. Among the various ecological issues, one alarming issue is the water crisis being faced by the world.

Water pollution is a serious problem, and learning how to identify, take care of, and prevent it is more important with every

---

[175] Augustine Thottakara, "Introduction," in *Eco-Spirituality – Perspectives from World Religions*, edited by Augustine Thottakara (Rome: Centre for Indian and Inter-Religious Studies, 1995), vii-viii.

passing year. The increasing pollution of water is the primary global risk in terms of its overwhelming global impact on society. Human beings are guilty of exploiting this natural resource to such an extent that controlling pollution has become a Herculean task. Pollution of water is making water scarcity a larger threat even for the future generations.

What is the role of religion in humanity's care of water and the global water crisis? The World Scientists' Warning to Humanity has called upon the assistance of the world's religious leaders to resolve the critical global water crisis. The WCC's "Justice, Peace, Creation" campaign, is especially concerned with ecology and climate change. In 2000, the world's religious leaders met at the UN and signed the "Commitment to Global Peace." This included a call to protect the environment for the present as well as future generations.[176] As the world faces the challenge of sustaining the world's water for the present and future generations, religion continues to play an increasingly acknowledged ethical and practical role.

In such a global scenario, from among the world's living religions, Zoroastrianism one of the oldest religion is one such religion in whose teachings and traditions water holds a pivotal place. Therefore, the significance of water in Zoroastrianism seems to have certain relevance for today. Zoroastrianism, although practiced and followed by a handful of people is one of the most interesting religions of the world and Rev. Dr. C. A. B. Tirkey opines that it merits our study because of the central dignity of the prophet Zoroaster/Zarathustra's preaching and because of the influence that some scholars suppose it has had.[177]

1. H_2o-Pocalypse Facing the World

Water is an essential part of life not only to quench thirst or for health. Water is crucial for creating jobs and supporting income,

---

[176] http://www.waterencyclopedia.com/Po-Re/Religions-Water-in.html (March 8, 2018).

[177] Christopher Augustus Bixel Tirkey, *Major Religions of India* (Delhi: ISPCK, 2001), 463. Hereafter cited as Tirkey, *Major Religions...*

social and human development. Water is a vital necessity of life, hence the aggravating warnings regarding water scarcity and an imminent global water catastrophe is extremely concerning for world leaders.

The issue of water scarcity was first raised in the United Nations Conference on Environment and Development held at Rio de Janeiro in 1992.[178] After the declaration of 22nd March as World Day for Water, a specific theme has been selected each year and the theme for 2018 was "Nature for Water" and it explores how nature can be utilized to overcome the water challenges of the 21st century.[179]

Cities across the world are becoming increasingly thirsty as the demand for water grows and supply decreases. All over the world scientists are presenting gloomy predictions. Groundwater is being pumped so aggressively that land is sinking. Some neighbourhoods in Beijing (the world's fifth most water-stressed city) are sinking at as much as 10 centimeters a year. The World Bank forecasts that water availability in cities could decline by as much as two thirds by 2050, according to the World Economic Forum's 2017 Global Risks Report.[180] Research shows that at the

---

[178] The United Nations General Assembly adopted resolution A/RES/47/193 on 22 December 1992 by which 22 March of each year was declared World Day for Water, to be observed starting in 1993, in conformity with the recommendations of the United Nations Conference on Environment and Development (UNCED) contained in Chapter 18 (Fresh Water Resources) of Agenda 21. States were invited to devote the Day, as appropriate in the national context, to concrete activities such as the promotion of public awareness through the publication and diffusion of documentaries and the organization of conferences, round tables, seminars and expositions related to the conservation and development of water resources and the implementation of the recommendations of Agenda 21. https://en.unesco.org/themes/water-security/world-water-day, (February 26, 2018).

[179] http://www.un.org/en/events/waterday/, (February 26, 2018).

[180] http://www.un.org/en/events/waterday/, (February 26, 2018).

current rate of consumption, two-thirds of the world's population will be facing water shortages as a daily reality by 2025.[181]

With special reference to India, the huge population makes her very vulnerable when it comes to water shortage and scarcity. About 330 million people in the country now suffer from regular water shortage issues. A dry spell causes the number of people suffering to rise sharply. A recent study suggests that by 2040 there will be no drinking water in almost all of India. Between 2030 and 2040, many parts of the world will face fresh water scarcity and India is likely to be one of the worst affected countries. The statistics concerning the water shortage in India is indeed alarming:[182]

- Per capita availability of water in India has gone down from 6,042 cubic metre in 1947 to about 1,545 cubic metre in 2011.
- By 2050, India's burgeoning population and water scarcity will reach alarming proportions.
- Over 90 percent of the waste water discharged into rivers, lakes, and ponds is untreated and leads to further contamination of fresh water sources.
- The greatest waste of fresh water comes from lack of adequate storage and utilisation facilities of river waters.
- India has no desalination facilities to use the abundant seawater resources.

2. Water Scarcity and Its Implications

The water crisis holds various implications for the world ranging from economic and health issues to peace and stability of nations

---

[181] Prof Young a specialist in water policy reform who holds a Research Chair in Water and Environmental Policy at the University of Adelaide says that, "What's happening bit by bit is that water scarcity is becoming increasingly common all around the world, no matter where you look as country after country hits the limit of what it can use." http://www.news.com.au/technology/environment/conservation/the-approaching-crisis-is-the-world-running-out-of-water/news-story/8d48f0cce7b33bc7b480d8e6f1e9152b, (February 26, 2018).

[182] https://www.mapsofindia.com/my-india/india/world-water-day-2017-indias-wake-up-call (February 26, 2018).

all around the world. Therefore, the water crisis being faced by the world is an issue that cannot be ignored any longer.

2.1. Economic Implications: Among the economic implications of water scarcity is the impact on businesses worldwide leading to higher operating costs and staying competitive. Water scarcity will inevitably result in difficulty of controlling costs. This will further result in firms relocating to areas where water is abundant, such as cities located by a lake, river, or river basin. This will ultimately have a domino effect on communities: local commerce declines, incomes go down, tax revenues decrease, population declines due to lack of employment opportunities, cities and the surrounding communities shrink dangerously.[183]

Another significant economic implication of water scarcity is the effect on agriculture. The decreasing water resources means environmental deterioration and land use loss for agricultural purposes. Reduction in farm crop production will result in extreme spike in food prices. Increase in food prices and water scarcity leads to regional conflicts and migration of people to places where water is abundant. Water scarcity further leads to food shortages and rise in food prices which lead to hindering of trade with developing economies and in the long run can cause civil unrest.[184]

2.2. Health Implications: Twenty million people are facing famine in Somalia, South Sudan, Yemen and northern Nigeria, partly as a result of severe drought over recent years and general mismanagement of water. There is a direct link between water quality and health. The WASH Poverty Diagnostics demonstrate that poor water and sanitation is a major contributing factor to stunting in children. Children who suffer from malnutrition, dirty water and disease don't develop properly and, as a result, are caught with stunted brain development for the rest of their lives,

---

[183] https://globalriskinsights.com/2016/12/economic-cost-global-water-scarcity/ (March 6, 2018).

[184] https://globalriskinsights.com/2016/12/economic-cost-global-water-scarcity/ (March 6, 2018).

translating into lesser job opportunities and incomes. They don't get a second chance at living their lives to the fullest potential. There are still over 3 billion people who lack basic access to clean water and proper sanitation – of those, 663 million people lack access to drinking water; 2.4 billion people lack access to improved sanitation and 1.1 billion still practice open defecation, spreading disease.[185]

2.3. Implications on International Security: One of the major factors causing the global water crisis is bad managing – water is wasted almost everywhere, in agriculture, industry or domestic use. In addition to obvious health issues, water scarcity has serious implications on (international) security.

The United Nations Secretary-General Antonio Guterres warned that by 2050 global demand for fresh water is projected to grow by more than 40 per cent and at least a quarter of the world's population will live in countries with a "chronic or recurrent" lack of clean water. He told the UN Security Council that "strains on water access are already rising in all regions" and it was causing tension between nations. Water scarcity is a serious challenge in many countries and it accentuates already fragile situations and causes further conflict and violence.[186] Unrest, instability and conflict can all be triggered or worsened by water scarcity. Besides the inefficient management of water, it is also distributed unevenly across the world, making some regions more stressed.[187]

---

[185] http://www.worldbank.org/en/news/feature/2017/03/22/world-water-day-2017 (February 26, 2018).

[186] http://www.news.com.au/technology/environment/conservation/the-approaching-crisis-is-the-world-running-out-of-water/news-story/8d48f0cce7b33bc7b480d8e6f1e9152b (February 26, 2018).

[187] Among the various stressed regions, the Middle East will be one of the most affected. In addition, the US National Intelligence Council has identified South Asia and North Africa as regions that will face substantial water problems and increased risk of instability and state failure. In these regions, water and politics are closely intertwined. Shared waters often cause disputes, as they are connected with states' vital interests. Some countries expressed willingness to go to war over their rivers. Such is the case of Egypt, whose president said already in 1979: "The only matter that could take Egypt to war again is water." Without

Moving to the Middle East, among the many wars in this area not one was waged solely over water, but water scarcity has aggravated other factors leading to conflict. The civil war in Syria has been re-classified by many as a climate-change war erupting as a result of the protracted drought in the country between 2006 and 2011. Israeli-Palestinian conflict can also be linked to water. Israel has control over most resources of fresh water and is using this as a tool of domination over Palestinians, denying thousands in the occupied West Bank access to water and preventing them from developing their water infrastructure, leaving them water-dependent. In addition to disputed territories, water will be the main obstacle to reaching a peaceful solution.[188]

Similarly, water has been cause of tension between two 'mortal' enemies, India and Pakistan with regards to the shared waters of the Indus River. Pakistan relies heavily on the Indus River and its streams for water and food supply as well as electricity production. In 1960, the Indus Waters Treaty was signed. However, in recent years, this otherwise successful water treaty is challenged due to the rapid growth of population and increased use of water in agriculture and industry. Two states in perpetual conflict since their creation, armed with nuclear

---

the Nile there would be no Egypt. Hence, the Ethiopian decision to build a dam over the river enraged the Egyptians, since the Ethiopian Renaissance Dam could potentially cut the flow of the Nile to Egypt and thus cause great damage to its economy. With the signing of an agreement between Egypt, Ethiopia and Sudan in 2015, war seems unlikely at the moment. However, there is no doubt that the Nile will continue to stir the relations between the countries through which it flows. Water Crisis and its Impact on International Security: Water Scarcity as the Next Great Driver of Conflicts, https://www.iapss.org/wp/2017/02/09/water-crisis-and-its-impact-on-international-security-water-scarcity-as-the-next-great-driver-of-conflicts/ (March 6, 2018).

[188] https://www.iapss.org/wp/2017/02/09/water-crisis-and-its-impact-on-international-security-water-scarcity-as-the-next-great-driver-of-conflicts/ (March 6, 2018).

weapons, are at constant loggerheads and the threat of a nuclear conflict over water looms in the air.[189]

3. Water in Religion

Water in religion is not a mere word. In fact, it is a symbol which is shared by all the world's religions and which plays a vital role in the rituals. Religions have recognized the sacredness of water since time immemorial because it is the basis for all life. Water has a central place in the practices and beliefs of many religions for two main reasons. Firstly, water is venerated because of its cleansing attribute which is believed to wash away impurities and pollution and make an object as good as new. Water not only purifies objects for ritual use, but can make a person clean, externally or spiritually, ready to come into the presence of his/her focus of worship.

Secondly, water is the basis of life and without water there is no life. However, water has the power to destroy as well as to create. We are at the mercy of water just as we are at the mercy of our God or gods. The significance of water manifests itself differently in different religions and beliefs but it is these two qualities of water that underlie its place in our cultures and faiths.

Water is a common element found in many accounts of the creation of the world. In some accounts, the creator remains independent, while in others the creator is part of the waters. Water may also be a representation of the divine. It may signify nothingness, contain some substance from which the Earth or life is created, or have spontaneous life-generating power of its own. The idea of a firmament separating upper (heaven) and lower (earth) waters also appear in many religions. Rivers and lakes may separate the world of the living from the dead. Almost all religions speak of a flood account. In some traditions the flood is meant for the punishment of humankind. In some it is a result of

---

[189] https://www.iapss.org/wp/2017/02/09/water-crisis-and-its-impact-on-international-security-water-scarcity-as-the-next-great-driver-of-conflicts/ (March 6, 2018).

fighting among the gods. Furthermore, water is also associated with cleansing and purification of body and spirit.[190]

Hence, we can say that in different religious traditions, the image of water has been given a wide range of meaning. These diverse and sometimes opposing meanings are to a large extent due to the diversity of our experience of water as a natural phenomenon. Water can symbolize a formless material that the gods may use to fulfill their purpose. It bathes, dissolves, and purifies. Essential to all life forms, it symbolizes a generative or life-giving quality, very similar to creative power. Thus, it is divine and sacred. However, as has been mentioned earlier, water also has the potential of playing a negative role. In the hands of the gods, the destructive power of its waves may be utilized to wreak havoc. Since active in itself, whether divine or monstrous, water erodes everything that takes form and tends to annihilate all distinctions in its own inconsistency.[191]

4. Zoroastrianism: The 'Good Religion'

Nicol McNicol opines that, of all the ancient religions which have a continuous history and survive as living faiths till today, there is none that has so small a company of adherents as Zoroastrianism.[192] Nevertheless, considering the small number of followers of this particular religion, the impact that it has made on the world is relatively large. Zoroastrianism is a unique religion which emphasizes the eternal battle between good and evil. The founder of Zoroastrianism was Zoroaster (a Greek corruption of the Old Iranian word *Zarathushtra*). His time and place of birth are unknown, but it is generally believed that he was born around

---

[190] http://www.waterencyclopedia.com/Po-Re/Religions-Water-in.html (March 8, 2018).

[191] Jean Rudhardt, "Water," in *Encyclopedia of Religion,* edited by Mircea Eliade, vol. 15 (New York: Mcmillan Publishing Company, 1987), 350-358.

[192] Nicol Macnicol, *The Living Religions of the Indian People* (New Delhi: Oriental Books Reprint Corporation, 1979), 326. Hereafter cited as Macnicol, *Living Religions...*

650 B.C.E in Persia.[193] Ninian Smart on the other hand asserts that according to Zoroastrian sources; Zoroaster lived 300 years (or less) before Alexander the Great which places him around 630 B.C.E. Smart further opines that there is a consensus among scholars that Zoraoster was much older than that and he was probably of the tenth century B.C.E.[194]

Zoroastrianism has often been called the 'good religion' because of its emphasis on goodness and on religious thought and behavior. It is the outcome of a prophetic reformation of the old polytheistic Iranian religion which in many ways is comparable to the work of the Israelite prophets. In fact, Zoroastrianism has many points of resemblance to the Old Testament.[195] Stressing on the ethical principles taught by Zoroastrianism, Prof. A. V. Williams Jackson, one of the most authoritative of the scholars who have studied this subject categorically states that, "The sacred books of but few peoples contain so clear a grasp of right and wrong, or so ethical a conception of duty, as the Zoroastrian scriptures…"[196]

This faith is still professed by the Parsis of Mumbai and by some sporadic communities in Persia. Although, adherents are spread worldwide, they do not constitute a significant number. The total number of currently practicing adherents of Zoroastrianism is unknown.[197]

---

[193] Josh McDowell and Don Stewart, *Handbook of Today's Religions* (Nashville: Thomas Nelson Publishers, 1983), 356.

[194] Ninian Smart, *The World's Religions: Old Traditions and Modern Transformation* (Cambridge: Cambridge University Press, 1992), 215.

[195] V. S. Lalrinawma, *Major Faith Traditions of India* (Delhi: ISPCK, 2007), 339.

[196] Macnicol, *Living Religions…,* 326.

[197] In 2012 the FEZANA Journal, a quarterly publication of the Federation of Zoroastrian Associations of North America (FEZANA), had published a demographic picture of Zoroastrians around the world and a comparison with a similar study done in the year, 2004. According to this study, Total World Zoroastrian Population is 1,11,691 if we use best estimated population for Iran. If we use the 2011 census figures for Iran, the Total World Population is 1,21,962 Zoroastrians. Roshan Rivetna, "The Zarathushti World, a 2012 Demographic Picture," FEZANA Journal, Fall 2013. www.fezana.org.

5. Significance of Water in Zoroastrianism

The ancient Iranians greatly respected waters and the smallest spring or dewdrop was regarded as representing the whole creation of water. The great respect of the ancient Iranians for the waters was also acknowledged by both the Greeks and the Romans, who both reported how the Persians took great efforts through elaborate rituals to maintain the waters from pollution. Accordingly, the ancient Iranians evidently made offerings to waters, to keep them pure and vivifying.[198]

Rustom Masani is of the opinion that Zoroastrians have imbibed their veneration of water from their Aryan ancestors. One might as well regard Zoroastrians as water-worshippers, because they recite their prayers before the waters of wells, springs, and seas. However, such adoration or veneration does not imply that the object adored is considered to be the Supreme Deity.[199] Zoroastrianism preaches a strict monotheism. According to Zoroaster, *Ahura Mazda* is the only God whom people should adore and worship. However, the Zoroastrians also believe in the six *Amesha Spentas* (the Bounteous Immortals) who are worthy of worship. Nevertheless, the *Amesha Spentas* are not considered wholly separate from *Ahura* Mazda.[200]

Amesha Spentas, with God's Holy Spirit, *Spenta Mainyu* are linked with God's creation. The *Amesha Spentas* are believed to dwell within each of their creations while at the same time remaining aspects of God's nature. Each *Amesha Spenta* protects

---

198 https://authenticgathazoroastrianism.org/2011/10/28/192/ (March 5, 2018).

199 Rustom Masani, *The Religion of the Good Life* (London: George Allen & Unwin Ltd., 1938), 86-88.

200 Many attributes are given to *Ahura Mazda*. It is taught that *Ahura Mazda* reveals himself to humankind through six different modes, known as the *Amesha Spentas* (the Bounteous Immortals/ Holy Immortals). These six modes are considered as the six aspects of the Supreme God through which he reveals himself. They may also be regarded as the six archangels through whom *Ahura Mazda* reveals himself to people. These six aspects or archangels are *Asha, Vohu Manah, Kshathra, Armaiti, Haurvatat and Ameretat.* Tirkey, *Major Religions*..., 481.

its creation and represents an aspect of *Ahura Mazda* and a feature of the good creation. These creations are the means by which worshippers can approach *Ahura Mazda* and by which *Ahura Mazda* can approach his worshippers. *Haurvatat* (meaning wholeness, health and integrity) is a feminine being and the creator of water and is represented by consecrated water used in priestly acts of worship. In everyday life *Haurvatat* is observed by keeping water unpolluted and being temperate and self-disciplined.[201]

In Zoroastrianism, polluting of water is considered 'sin.' The *Arda Wiraz-Namag*[202] mentions several sins such as neglecting menstrual restrictions which includes approaching water or fire during menstruation, washing in (and thereby polluting) lakes or springs, polluting public bathhouses, not giving water to farm animals etc. According to Zoroastrian tradition, when the world was created the Evil Spirit *Angra Mainyu* attacked the earth and among other things made pure water salty. As mentioned earlier, Zoroastrians believe that pollution is evil and that water, when pure, is sacred. Zoroastrians themselves must avoid pollution of any kind and must perform ritual ablutions before saying their prayers (which are said 5 times a day facing a source of light) and before any religious ceremonies such as weddings.[203]

The significance of water in Zoroastrianism is a combination of its purifying properties and its importance as a fundamental life element. Therefore, while water is used in purification rites and rituals it is sacred by itself and so must be kept from being polluted. Water, because of its sacredness should never be drawn

---

[201] http://www.rainharvest.co.za/2011/04/water-in-religion-part-3/ (March 5, 2018).

[202] The *Arda Wiraz-Namag* is Wiraz's journey into heaven, hell, and purgatory and his description of the rewards and punishments for given actions that he had witnessed there. The *Arda Wiraz-Namag* is thus a literary catalogue of the actions considered as *winah* and their consequences in the afterlife. Michael Stausberg and Yuhan Sohrab-Dinshaw Vevaina, eds., *The Wiley Blackwell Companion to Zoroastrianism* (West Sussex, UK: John Wiley & Sons, Ltd., 2015), 325.

[203] http://www.africanwater.org/religion.htm#Zoroastrianism (March 5, 2018).

from a well or a stream during hours of darkness. Holy water prepared through a particular ritual is an important element of Zoroastrianism. However, this holy water should be prepared between sunrise and noon. Furthermore, to pray or meditate next to streams, rivers, waterfalls, springs, lakes, seas and the ocean is highly recommended in Zoroastrianism. Therefore, on the 10th day of each Zoroastrian month, the believers make a pilgrimage to various sources of water and offer their respect and prayers to the waters. It is believed that through the offering of prayers and respect to the waters, the vital creation of water which sustains all living things, is made stronger, purer and more abundant.

According to Zoroastrian teachings, water and fire are to be looked to with care and reverence, because they are instruments of purification. Further, such sacred elements as fire and water should not be polluted through contact with impure things such as a dead body.[204] Hence, in Zoroastrianism, the dead are neither immersed in water nor are they buried. They are taken to a mountain where there is the 'Tower of Silence' a roofless construction. Here the dead body is kept and birds of prey swoop down upon the corpse and strip it to the bones.

Since Zoroastrianism gives so much significance to water, the punishment for polluting wells or water in general is also very severe. If a person leaves a well uncovered so that the corpse eating dogs and birds carry the bones to the water and the trees, his sin amounts to "*tanafiir*." If a person who has touched a corpse touches water and trees without being cleansed the punishment amounts to four hundred stripes. If a person deliberately carries dead matter to water and fire, that person is worthy of death. If any person shall sow or water, within a year, the piece of ground where dog and men have died, they are "*Peshotanus*" (one who pays with his body or worthy of death).[205] Therefore, there are special rules concerning water and fire which are particular to the faith.

---

[204] Maganlal A. Buch, *Zoroastrian Ethics* (Baroda: A.G. Widgery, 1919), 102-103. Herafter cited as Buch, *Zoroastrian Ethics*...

[205] Buch, *Zoroastrian Ethics...,* 174-175.

Most people use water recklessly for washing; but for a Zoroastrian the cleanliness of water itself is to be protected, since it is the creation of *Haurvatat*. So, nothing impure should be allowed in direct contact with a natural source of water, such as lake, stream or well. If anything ritually unclean is to be washed, water should be drawn off for this purpose, and even then, this is not to be used directly, but the impure object should first be cleaned with cattle-urine, and then dried with sand or in sunlight before water is allowed to touch it for the final washing.[206]

6. Relevance of Water in Zoroastrianism for the Global Water Crisis

The world's thirst for water is likely to become one of the most pressing resource issues of the 21st Century. Research indicates that, global water consumption rose six-fold between 1900 and 1995, more than double the rate of population growth. If we continue business as usual (increasing population, water usage, pollution and wastage) it is estimated that by the year 2030 the global water demand for freshwater will exceed the supply. Currently more than one-third of the world's population experiences serious water problems and polluted water sickens more than 1 billion people each year. Water pollution adds enormously to existing problems of water scarcity by contaminating large volumes of available water, thus making it unsuitable for use. This situation is worst in third world countries, where human health is gravely damaged by accelerating contamination of water supplies by eutrophication, heavy metals, persistent organic pollutants, acidification and sewage pollution.[207]

It is in such a context that the Zoroastrian teaching on maintaining the purity of water and water bodies hold much relevance. The Zoroastrian outlook on their relationship with

---

[206] Mary Boyce, *Zoroastrians: Their Religious Beliefs and Practices* (London: Routledge & Kegan Paul Ltd., 1979), 43-44.

[207] http://www.environment.nsw.gov.au/stormwater/HSIEteachguide/WaterPoln.htm (March 5, 2018).

the natural world has led the community to work on forestry and water-related issues. According to Zoroastrianism, humanity's role in this world is to serve and honor the Wise Lord as well as the Seven Bounteous Creations – the sky, water, earth, plants, animals, humankind, and fire – which are the gifts of God to humankind.

The following important points may be inferred from the concept and significance of water in Zoroastrianism which holds relevance for today's context:

6.1. Water is a Gift to Humanity from the Creator: The uniqueness of the Zoroastrian faith is that caring for the physical world is not only to seek spiritual salvation, since human beings are the purposeful creation of God, they are the natural overseers of the Seven Creations endowed with the task of caring for the universe. This endorses caring for the Seven Creations as part of a symbiotic relationship.[208] Water according to Zoroastrian teaching is sacred and it is the good creation of the Supreme Being, *Ahura Mazda*. Therefore, water is not considered to be the property of an individual, a community or the state, it is a gift of God. Since the world and everything in it is the creation of God, He alone is the sole owner and human beings are only the care-takers. In the near future, water scarcity and the impending water crisis may create a situation where water may be monopolized and privatized by individuals and nations. A stage may come when water may become a more expensive commodity than oil and gold combined. However, the teachings of Zoroastrianism reiterate that water is a gift of God to humankind for their sustenance. It is neither the property of individuals nor the state.

6.2 Water is Not to Be Polluted: Zoroastrianism considers pollution as the work of *Angra Mainyu*. Therefore, it is a sin to pollute water which is the creation of God, *Ahura Mazda*. As such, Zoroastrianism teaches that human beings should never urinate or defecate in water. It is a Zoroastrian tradition to never enter a river to wash in it or pollute it in any way. The wedding liturgy also

---

[208] Paula R. Hartz, *World Religions: Zoroastrianism* (New York: Chelsea House Publishers, 2009), 137. Hereafter cited as Hartz, *Zoroastrianism*...

specifically reminds newlyweds that they carry a duty to maintain the purity of running water. One of the major reasons for the global water crisis is as a result of water pollution. The pollution of water through dumping of waste, human excrements etc., is creating shortage of clean drinking water, and having serious health implications. In such a context, the Zoroastrian teaching on maintaining the purity of water holds much relevance. In fact, Zoroastrianism believes that respect and adoration of the vital creation of water which sustains all living things, will make it stronger, purer and more abundant. Therefore, the world, realizing the value of water and its essentiality for life should learn to pay more respect so that every nation and tribe will have enough water to drink and sustain their lives.

6.3. Water is to Be Well-Managed: Much of the water crisis facing the world is due to mismanagement of water. Although, it is true that water is a renewable resource, it is often wasted – in agriculture, industry or domestic use. Moreover, as we pollute our available water at an alarming rate, we also fail to treat it. About 80 percent of the world's wastewater is discharged back into nature without further treatment or reuse. Zoroastrianism, which teaches and believes in the sacredness of water, teaches us that maintaining the purity of water will make it purer and stronger, replenishing the resources so that everyone will have enough. It also teaches us the judicious use of water which is the gift of the Supreme God.

6.4. A Just Society is An Eco-just Society: The creation of a just society in Zoroastrianism also extends to the ecological sphere, due to the immense importance placed upon nature. Many important Zoroastrian festivals, including the *Ghambars*, honor the majesty of the natural world. Further, care for the planet is necessary for all who wish to become *ashavans* (one who possesses truth/righteousness), and protecting the environment is seen as a precursor for the refurbishment of earth that will take place at *frashokereti* (the Zoroastrian doctrine of a final renovation of the universe, when evil will be destroyed, and everything else will be then in perfect unity with God).[209] Zoroastrianism sees the physical world as a natural matrix of Seven Creations in which life and growth are interdependent if harmony and perfection are the final goal. This goal is to be achieved by re-creating the primeval unity of a perfect world, unpolluted and unsullied, as was first conceived by *Ahura Mazda*, the Wise Lord.[210]

Conclusion

Gary Chamberlain asserts that,

> "religious meanings must be considered in developing approaches to the global water crisis. Religions shape our understandings of who we are and how we relate to the natural world. We are in desperate need of new world views, new "cosmologies," or views of the universe, particularly a *new ethos* around water, to guide our decisions for the present as well as future uses of natural resources."[211]

Religion alone may be insufficient to solve water issues. However, they can go a long way in shaping people's understandings, involvement, and motivations in making the necessary, even revolutionary changes to develop a new water ethic. At the same time, the water crisis being faced by the world challenges religious traditions to engage in reshaping our basic responses to this profoundly real as well as symbolic place of water. In such a situation, the Zoroastrian religious tradition, one of the oldest living religion of the world and its teachings concerning water challenges each and every one of us to do our part in maintaining the purity and sanctity of water, which is vital for the sustenance of every life-form on this earth and for the survival of the earth itself.

---

[209] http://www.newworldencyclopedia.org/entry/Zoroastrianism (March 5, 2018).

[210] Hartz, *Zoroastrianism...,* 137.

[211] Gary Chamberlain, *Troubled Waters: Religion, Ethics, and the Global Water Crisis* (Maryland, US: Rowman & Littlefield, 2008), 4.

Bibliography

Dictionaries & Encyclopedias

Bhattacharya, N. N. *Jainism A Concise Encyclopaedia*. New Delhi: Manohar Publishers & Distributors, 2009.

Bisht, Narendra S. and T. S. Bankoti. Eds. *Encyclopaedic Ethnography of the Himalayan Tribes: A-D, Volume 1*. Delhi: Global Vision Pub House, 2004.

Cole, W. Owen and Piara Singh Sambhi. *A Popular Dictionary of Sikhism.* Curzon Press: Surrey, 1997.

Newby, Gordon D. *A Concise Encyclopedia of Islam*. Oxford, England: Oneworld Publications, 2002.

Rudhardt, Jean. "Water." In *Encyclopedia of Religion.* Edited by Mircea Eliade, vol. 15. New York: Mcmillan Publishing Company, 1987: 350-358.

Soanes, Catherine. Ed., et. al. *Compact Oxford Dictionary, Thesaurus, and Wordpower Guide*. Oxford: Oxford University Press, Indian Edition, 15th Impression, 2005.

Books & Journals

Abir, A. Peter. Ed. *Biblical Apostolate and Religious Fundamentalism*. Chennai: Catholic Bishop Federation, 2004.

Adamec, Ludwig W. *The A-to-Z of Islam*. New Delhi: Vision Books Pvt. Ltd., 2003.

Anand, Subhash. *Major Hindu Festivals: A Christian Appreciation*. Bombay: St. Paul Publications, 1991.

Augustine, John S. Ed. *Religious Fundamentalism: An Asian Perspective*. Bangalore: SATHRI/CCA/WARC, 1993.

Baltazar, Stella. 'Religious Fundamentalism: A Feminist Perspective.' In John S. Augustine, ed., *Religious Fundamentalism: An Asian Perspective*. Bangalore: SATHRI/CCA/WARC, 1993.

Barbato, Melanie. *Jain Approaches to Plurality: Identity as Dialogue*. Netherlands: Brill, 2018.

Bhargava, P. L. *Fundamentals of Hinduism: A Rational Analysis*. New Delhi: Munshiram Manoharlal Publishers Pvt. Ltd., 1982.

Bouquet, A. C. *Hinduism*. London: Hutchinson and Co (Publishers) Ltd., 1949.

Boyce, Mary. *Zoroastrians: Their Religious Beliefs and Practices*. London: Routledge & Kegan Paul Ltd., 1

Buch, Maganlal A. *Zoroastrian Ethics*. Baroda: A. G. Widgery, 1919.

Chamberlain, Gary. *Troubled Waters: Religion, Ethics, and the Global Water Crisis*. Maryland, US: Rowman & Littlefield, 2008.

Chatterjee, Satischandra and Dhirendramohan Datta. *An Introduction to Indian Philosophy*. New Delhi: Rupa Publications India Private Limited, 2007.

Chaudhuri, Nirad C. *Hinduism: A Religion to Live By*. New Delhi: B.I. Publications, 1979.

Daniel, P. S. "The Jaina Religious Tradition." In *Religious Traditions of India*. Edited by P. S. Daniel, David C. Scott and G. R. Singh. Delhi: ISPCK, 1988.

Donaldson, Dwight M. *Studies in Muslim Ethics*. London: SPCK, 1953.

Dwivedi, R. C. Ed. *Contribution of Jainism to Indian Culture*. Delhi: Motilal Banarsidass, 1975.

Eliade, Mircea. *Myth and Reality.* London: George Allen and Unwin Ltd., 1963.

Engineer, Asghar Ali. "Islamic Fundamentalism and Communalism in India." In *Religion and Asian Politics: An Islamic Perspective*. Hong Kong: Christian Conference of Asia-International Affairs, 1985.

Flood, Gavin. *An Introduction to Hinduism*. New Delhi: Cambridge University Press, 2004.

Gaikwad, Roger. "Why Study Religions? Reclaiming Religions in the Context of Religious Fundamentalism." In Lalchawiliana Varte and K. Lalchhuanawma. Eds. *Religion and Women: Pilgrims in Search of Justice and Equity*. Aizawl: Lengchhawn Press, 2018.

Gopalan, S. *Outlines of Jainism.* New Delhi: Wiley Eastern Limited, 1975.

Hartz, Paula R. *World Religions: Zoroastrianism.* New York: Chelsea House Publishers, 2009.

Huart, A. "Hindu Calendar and Festivals." In *Religious Hinduism: A Presentation and Appraisal.* Edited by R. De Smet and J. Neuner. Mumbai: St. Pauls, 1964.

Jame'l, Mohammed Masjed. "The Monotheistic Vision of Man and Nature." In *Eco-Spirituality – Perspectives from World Religions.* Edited by Augustine Thottakara. Rome: Centre for Indian and Inter-Religious Studies, 1995.

Kaur, Surinder. "Equality of Women in Sikh Ideology." *Journal of Social Sciences Research, 6/2* (December 27, 2014): 1001-1003.

Kechutzar, Sashikaba. "Rethinking Naga Religious Traditions: An Exploration of Tribal Christian Spirituality." In *Theologizing Tribal Heritage – A Critical Re-Look.* Edited by Hrangthan Chhungi. Delhi: CWM/ISET-ECC/PCI/ISPCK, 2008.

Keitzer, Renthy. *In Search of a Relevant Gospel Message.* Guwahati: CLC, 1995.

Kher, V. B. Ed. *In Search of the Supreme,* 3 vols. Ahmedabad: Navajivan Publishing House, 1962.

Klostermaier, Klaus K. *A Survey of Hinduism.* United States of America: State University of New York Press, 2007.

_________. *Hinduism: A Short Introduction.* Oxford: Oneworld Publications, 2006.

Lalrinawma, V. S. *Major Faith Traditions of India.* Delhi: ISPCK, 2007.

_________. *Missiological Issues Facing the Contemporary Church in India.* Bangalore: Centre for Contemporary Christianity, 2011.

Lalsim, Ramdina. *Tribes of N.C. Hills, Assam.* Haflong: Cultural and Publicity Officer, N.C. Hills Autonomous Council, Haflong, Assam, 2005.

Longchar, A. Wati. "Myth: A Source for Conceptualising Tribal Theology." In *An Exploration of Tribal Theology.* Jorhat: The Tzudikong Baptist Church, 1997.

_________. *The Traditional Tribal Worldview and Modernity.* Jorhat: Eastern Theological College, 2000.

_________. *The Tribal Religious Traditions in North East India: An Introduction.* Jorhat: Eastern Theological College, 2000.

Macnicol, Nicol. *The Living Religions of the Indian People.* New Delhi: Oriental Books Reprint Corporation, 1979.

Mahadevan, T. M. P. *Outlines of Hinduism*. Bombay: Chetana Pvt. Ltd., 1954.

Masani, Rustom. *The Religion of the Good Life.* London: George Allen & Unwin Ltd., 1938.

McDowell, Josh and Don Stewart. *Handbook of Today's Religions.* Nashville: Thomas Nelson Publishers, 1983.

McLeod, W. H. *The A to Z of Sikhism.* Plymouth: Scarecrow Press, Inc., 2005.

Minz, Nirmal. "The study of Tribal Religion in India," in *Re-visioning India's Religious Traditions: Essays in Honour of Eric J. Lott*, edited by David C. Scott & Israel Selvanayagam. Delhi: ISPCK, 1996.

Nesbitt, Eleanor. *Sikhism A Very Short Introduction*. New York: Oxford University Press Inc., 2005.

Packer, J. I. *'Fundamentalism' and the Word of God*. Grand Rapids, Michigan: William B. Eerdmans Publishing Company, 1958.

Peschke, Karl H. *Christian Ethics Moral Theology in the Light of Vatican II*. Bangalore: Theological Publications in India, 1996.

Presler, Henry H. *Introducing strangers to Hinduism.* Allahabad: North India Christian Tract & Book Society, 1978.

_________. *Primitive Religions in India*. Bangalore: The Christian Literature Society, 1971.

Puthanangady, Paul. Challenges of Fundamentalism in Biblical Apostolate. In *Biblical Apostolate and Religious Fundamentalism*. Chennai: Catholic Bishop Federation, 2004.

Rahman, Fazlur. *Major Themes of the Qur'an.* Chicago: The University of Chicago Press, 2009.

Robinson, Gnana. "Why is Fundamentalism a Problem Today?." In *Fundamentalism and Secularism: The Indian Predicament.* Edited by Andreas Nehring. Madras: Gurukul Lutheran Theological College and Research Institute, 1994.

Samartha, Stanley J. "The Causes and Consequences of Religious Fundamentalism." In *Fundamentalism and Secularism: The*

Indian Predicament. Edited by Andreas Nehring. Madras: Gurukul Lutheran Theological College and Research Institute, 1994.

Sarkar, R. L. *The Bible, Ecology and Environment.* Delhi: ISPCK/ CISRS, 2000.

Scott, David C. The Hindu Religious Tradition. In *Religious Traditions of India*. Edited by P. S. Daniel, David C. Scott and G. R. Singh. New Delhi: ISPCK, 1988.

Sekhar, Vincent. *Quest for Harmony: An Anthology of Religions in Dialogue*. Bangalore: Claretian Publications, 2002.

Sengupta, Sarthak. Ed. *Tribal Studies in North East India*. New Delhi: Mittal Publication, 2002.

Sethia, Tara. *Ahimsā, Anekānta, and Jainism*. Delhi: Motilal Banarsidass Publishers, 2004.

Shah, Nagin J. Ed. *Jaina Theory of Multiple Facets of Reality and Truth (Anekāntavāda*). Delhi: Bhogilal Leharchand Institute of Indology, 2000.

_________. Trans. *Jaina Philosophy and Religion: English translation of Jaina Darsana by Munisri Nyayavijayaji*. Delhi: Bhogilal Lehar Chand Institute of Indology, 1998.

Shakespear, J. *The Lushei Kuki Clans Part I.* Aizawl: Tribal Research Institute, 1975.

Sharma, Chandradhar. *A Critical Survey of Indian Philosophy*. Delhi: Motilal Banarsidass Publishers, 1987.

Singh, Daljeet. *Essentials of Sikhism.* Singh Brothers: Amritsar, 1994.

Singh, Godwin R. "The Sikh Religious Tradition." In *Religious Tradition of India*. Edited by P. S. Daniel, David C. Scott and G. R. Singh. New Delhi: ISPCK, 1988.

Singh, N. K. *Islam – A Religion of Peace.* Delhi: Global Vision Publishing House, 2002.

Singh, Sardar Harjeet. *Faith and Philosophy of Sikhism.* Delhi: Kalpaz Publications, 2009.

Sinha, K. P. *The Philosophy of Jainism*. Calcutta: Punthi Pustak, 1990.

Smart, Ninian. *The World's Religions: Old Traditions and Modern Transformation*. Cambridge: Cambridge University Press, 1992.

Stausberg, Michael and Yuhan Sohrab-Dinshaw Vevaina. Eds. *The Wiley Blackwell Companion to Zoroastrianism*. West Sussex, UK: John Wiley & Sons, Ltd., 2015.

Tandon, Alok. "Anekantavada and Ahimsa: A Framework for Interreligious Dialogue," *Indian Philosophical Quarterly XXIX No I* (January 2002): 105-116.

Tayob, Abdulkader. *Islam – A Short Introduction*. Oxford, England: Oneworld Publications, 2006.

Thapar, Romila. *Interpreting Early India*. Delhi: Oxford University Press, 1993.

Thottakara, Augustine. "Introduction." In *Eco-Spirituality – Perspectives from World Religions*. Edited by Augustine Thottakara. Rome: Centre for Indian and Inter-Religious Studies, 1995.

Thumra, Jonathan H. "The Primal Religious Tradition." In *Religious Traditions of India.* Edited by P. S. Daniel, David C. Scott and G. R. Singh. Delhi: ISPCK, 2001.

Tirkey, Christopher Augustus Bixel. *Major Religions of India.* Delhi: ISPCK, 2001.

Vanlaltlani, T. *Tribal Religion: Mizo and Bru.* Aizawl: Mizo Theological Association, 2009.

Varte, Lalchawiliana. *Islam Sakhua Hi Eng Nge?* Aizawl: Sangthuami, 2019.

Vashum, Yangkahao. "Sources for Developing Tribal Theology." In *An Exploration of Tribal Theology*. Edited by Wati Longchar. Jorhat: The Tzudikong Baptist Church, 1997.

Verma, Rajeev. *Faith and Philosophy of Hinduism.* Delhi: Kalpaz Publications, 2009.

Vidyarthi, L. P. and Binay Kumar Rai. *The Tribal Culture of India.* New Delhi: Concept Publishing Company, 1976.

Weeraperuma, Susanaga. *Major Religions of India*. Delhi: Motilal Banarsidass Publishers, 1985.

Yulios, Geevarghese. *Message of Religions: Doing Theology with Asian Religious Resources*. Kolkata: PTCA/SCEPTRE, 2013.

Zawla, K. *Mizo Pi Pute leh an thlahte Chanchin*. Aizawl: K. Zawla, 1964.

Electronic Sources

http://environment-ecology.com/religion-and-ecology.html (29 July, 2017).

http://ezralalsim.blogspot.in/2011/01/biate.html (29 July 2013).

http://www.africanwater.org/religion.htm#Zoroastrianism (March 5, 2018).

http://www.crosscurrents.org/islamecology.htm (03 September 2013).

http://www.environment.nsw.gov.au/stormwater/HSIEteachguide/WaterPoln.htm (March 5, 2018).

http://www.hollys7.tripod.com/religionandecology.htm (01 September 2013).

http://www.merriam-webster.com/dictionary/myth (July 16, 2013).

http://www.news.com.au/technology/environment/conservation/the-approaching-crisis-is-the-world-running-out-of-water/news-story/8d48f0cce7b33bc7b480d8e6f1e9152b, (February 26, 2018).

http://www.newworldencyclopedia.org/entry/Folklore (July 16, 2013).

http://www.newworldencyclopedia.org/entry/Zoroastrianism (March 5, 2018).

http://www.rainharvest.co.za/2011/04/water-in-religion-part-3/ (March 5, 2018).

http://www.speednet.com.au/~keysar/ecology.htm (02 September 2013).

http://www.un.org/en/events/waterday/, (February 26, 2018).

http://www.waterencyclopedia.com/Po-Re/Religions-Water-in.html (March 8, 2018).

http://www.waterencyclopedia.com/Po-Re/Religions-Water-in.html (March 8, 2018).

http://www.worldbank.org/en/news/feature/2017/03/22/world-water-day-2017 (February 26, 2018).

https://authenticgathazoroastrianism.org/2011/10/28/192/ (March 5, 2018).

https://en.unesco.org/themes/water-security/world-water-day, (February 26, 2018).

https://en.wikipedia.org/wiki/Anekantavada (September 23, 2019).

https://globalriskinsights.com/2016/12/economic-cost-global-water-scarcity/ (March 6, 2018).

https://www.cry.org/issues-views/gender-inequality (29 March 2020).

https://www.cry.org/issues-views/gender-inequality (29 March 2020).

https://www.iapss.org/wp/2017/02/09/water-crisis-and-its-impact-on-international-security-water-scarcity-as-the-next-great-driver-of-conflicts/ (March 6, 2018).

https://www.learnreligions.com/sikhism-clergy-terms-meanings-4590180 (28 March, 2020).

https://www.mapsofindia.com/my-india/india/world-water-day-2017-indias-wake-up-call (February 26, 2018).

https://www.refworld.org/docid/49749d103c.html (17 March 2020).

https://www.un.org/sustainabledevelopment/gender-equality/ (29 March 2020).

https://www.undp.org/content/undp/en/home/sustainable-development-goals/goal-5-gender-equality.html (29 March 2020).

Personal telephone conversation with Mr. Ramdina Lalsim on 30 July 2013.

Roshan Rivetna. "The Zarathushti World, a 2012 Demographic Picture." FEZANA Journal, Fall 2013. www.fezana.org.